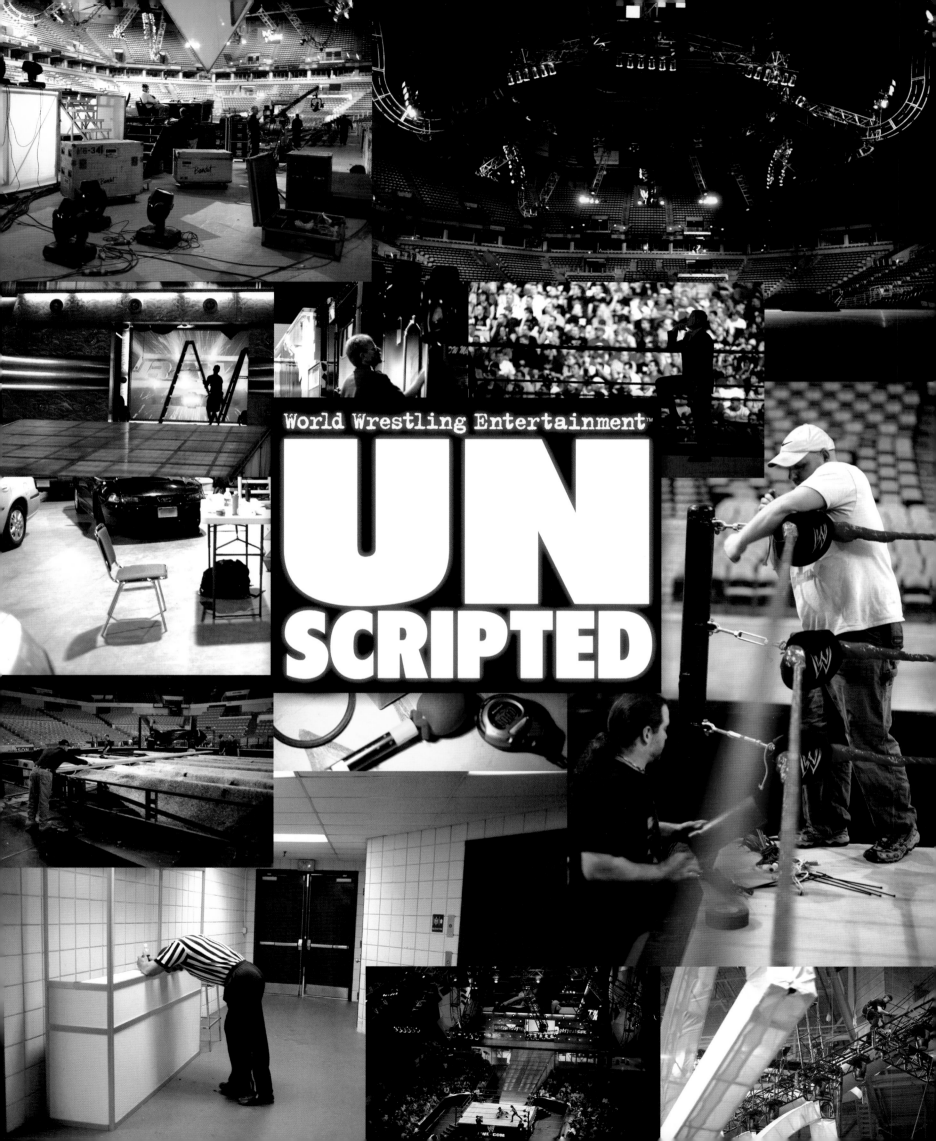

World Wrestling Entertainment™

UN SCRIPTED

World Wrestling Entertainment™

UN
SCRIPTED

EDITED BY

Ken Leiker and Mark Vancil

ART DIRECTION BY

Stacey Pascarella

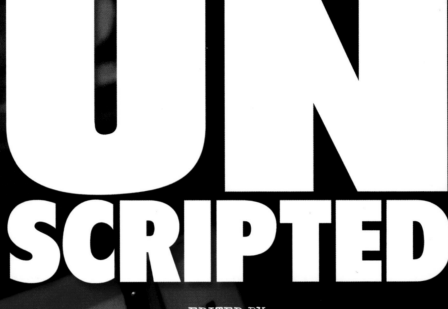

POCKET BOOKS

New York   London   Toronto   Sydney   Singapore

A LITTLE more than a year ago in the cramped quarters of a publishing office the concept for this book was conceived. We had an idea that involved individuals most of us only knew from television. What none of us had at that moment was a map defining the journey ahead. And what none of us at Rare Air Media knew at the time was just how wonderful that trip would become.

In the course of scheduling talent around an incredibly demanding lifestyle, securing imagery from vast archives and coordinating original interviews and photo sessions all over the country, the essential nature of an organization emerged. And it emerged through the passion, work ethic and innate goodness of every person at every level of World Wrestling Entertainment.

That it flows down hill from the top became clear in the late stages of this project when we talked to and photographed Vince and Linda McMahon and their family. But it all started with three remarkable people, Stacey Pascarella, Donna Goldsmith and Jim Ross. Donna welcomed us into the WWE world, Jim provided the blueprint and Stacey became our guide, conscience and collaborator. Though the daily demands of a complex entertainment company are self evident, never once would we have known they had another responsibility outside of this book. In working through a myriad of logistics — legal, personal and otherwise — Stacey's kindness and integrity never wavered. Jim simply dazzled us with his insight and assistance. The same could be said of the photo department where Noelle Carr and Frank Vitucci responded to every request at every hour of the day and night. Indeed, everyone listed below contributed in a way that exceeded any reasonable expectation. Last but not least, the WWE talent proved to be more unique than most of the rest of the world can imagine. The demands of their jobs - physically, mentally and psychologically — rival any professional sport anywhere on earth. The fact they understand and appreciate the importance of their fans speaks to the enduring appeal of the industry.

AT RARE AIR MEDIA | Nick De Carlo once again proved to be as wonderful a designer as he is a person. His talent and hard work can be found on every square inch of this book. As always, John Vieceli remains our godfather when it comes to design and production integrity. The words, insights and thoughts in this book are the product of countless hours of travel, interviews and research by Ken Leiker. In addition to being a remarkable editor and writer, Ken's compassion and integrity make him a truly special person. His friendship has only made these months more memorable. Much of the photography in this book is thanks to the hard work and creativity of Patrick Murphy-Racey. Patrick drove and flew thousands of miles often at the last moment to capture the men and women featured in this book. Like Ken, his ability proved to be matched only by his integrity.

AT SIMON & SCHUSTER | Scott Shannon and Margaret Clark proved to be among the finest people we have worked with in our 10 years in the publishing industry. Scott masks his brilliance with a kindness and compassion that smoothed every sharp edge and never made a single moment of this process seem like work. Margaret simply gets more done with less time than anyone we have ever had the pleasure of working with. Though she balanced dozens of other projects each with multiple demands, she very carefully took us through the most trying moments without complaint.

With a project of this size, there are always many more people deserving of mention.

AT WWE | All of the WWE Superstars, Mike Archer, Dave Barry, Ira Berg, Tom Bergamasco, Kasama Bhasathiti, Debbie Bonnanzio, Lynn Brent, Anthony Cali, Noelle Carr, Jill Clark, Bob Clarke, Ed Cohen, Donna Collins, Kate Cox, John D'Amico, Denise DeCesare, Debbie Degeralomo, Liz Difabio, Nicole Dorazio, Kevin Dunn, Rich Freeda, John Giamundo, Donna Goldsmith, Jennifer Good, Bernadette Hawks, Dave Hebner, Earl Hebner, Lisa Lee, Ed Kaufman, Linda McMahon, Marissa McMahon, Shane McMahon, Stephanie McMahon, Vince McMahon, Janice McNairn, Lauren Middlen, Virginia Mierisch, Bruce Prichard, Jim Ross, Ann Russo-Gordon, John Sohigian, Kevin Sullivan, Jessie Ward, Barry Werner, Andrew Wilson, Frank Vitucci, Janet Ventriglia, Veronica Zarrelli and Beth Zazza.

AT HOME | For my baby boy, Jonah William, who came into the world as this book was being created. As with your sisters Alexandra, Samantha and Isabella and your mother, my Laurita, the best of me comes from each of you. — Mark Vancil

To Cherié, James, Nicole, Courtney, and Taylor — the champions in my ring. — Ken Leiker

PHOTOGRAPHY

Craig Ambrosio	36 (Bottom), 38-39, 56-57, 62-63, 74-75, 92-93, 105-106, 172-173
Scott Brinegar	46, 192-193, 226-227
Henry DiRocco	8, 34, 45, 80, 102, 112-113, 126-127, 135 (Right), 156 (Center), 198
Rich Freeda	42, 44 (Center), 66-67, 84-85, 91, 96, 103, 114, 123, 129, 134-135 (Left), 138, 148, 152, 156 (Bottom), 158, 162, 164, 184-185, 190 (Bottom), 196-197, 212-213, 237
John Giamundo	21, 37, 83, 94, 100, 107, 115, 120-121, 138-139, 153, 175, 188, 189 (Top), 190-191, 236, 239
David Gunn	200-201
David McClain	35, 54-55, 86, 90
Craig Melvin	12-13, 30-31, 36 (Top), 44 (Bottom), 66-67, 72-73, 157, 170-171
Patrick Murphy-Racey	1-7, 10-11, 14-15, 17-19, 22-23, 26-29, 32-33, 40-41, 43-44 (Top), 47-53, 58-61, 64-65, 70-71, 76-79, 87-89, 95, 97-99, 101, 104, 108-111, 116, 118-119, 124-125, 128, 130, 132-133, 136-137, 140-147, 149, 154-155, 160-161, 163, 165-167, 176-181, 186-187, 194-195, 202-211, 214-225, 228-229, 230-235, 238, 240
Stacey Pascarella	183
Robert Reiff	117
2003 World Wrestling Entertainment, Inc.	16, 20, 168, 182

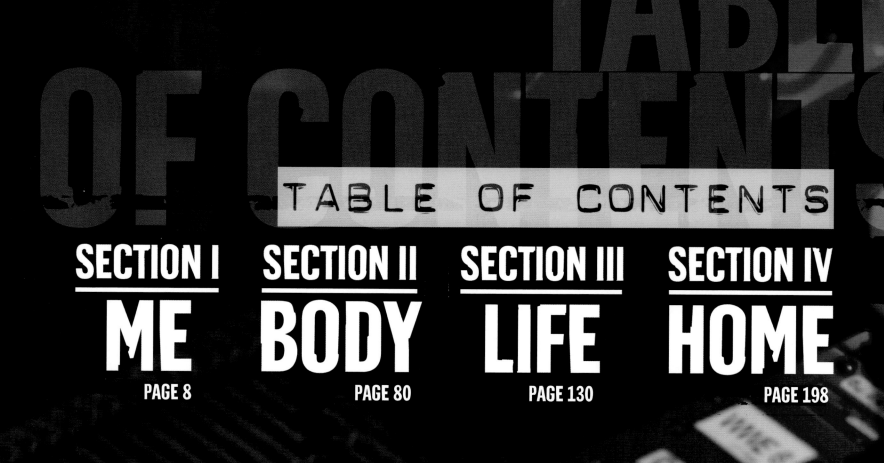

TABLE OF CONTENTS

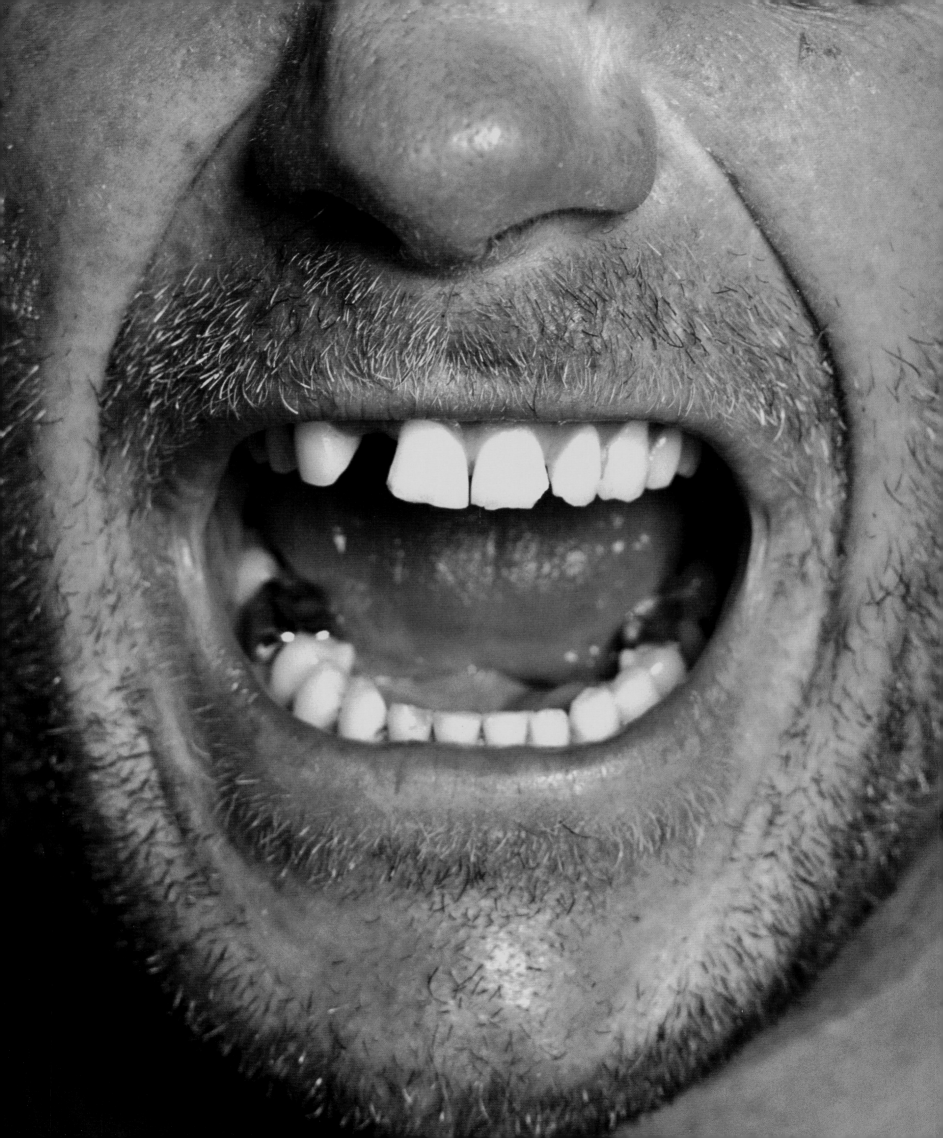

I WATCH WRESTLING TAPES ALL THE TIME FROM THE 1960s, 1970s, 1980s — WHATEVER I CAN GET.

Our company owns everything now, so I'm bugging the office all the time to put together tapes for me. I'll call the office and say, "Listen, I want the AWA tapes of Ray Stevens and Nick Bockwinkel as a tag team" — or whatever it is. I'll watch those tapes and pick things up. I don't watch for moves; I watch for the story they're telling, why they did things at a particular time. A lot of our guys today just don't understand the business. We all grew up as huge wrestling fans, and we need to understand why we liked it so much. It was because back then, they told stories, as opposed to just flip, flopping and flying. The guys that make the most money in our business have never been the guys that do moonsaults and jump off the top rope and do big dropkicks. It's the guys that tell the best stories that are in the main events, that are on top. We tell guys that all the time, and it's almost like the more we tell them, the more they try to go the other way.

The summer after my sophomore year, I put on

40 LBS OF

I HAD a real hard job that summer, digging ditches for a plumbing company. It was 8, 9, 10 hours a day. My growth hormones, testosterone, all that stuff started coming through for me, plus I had this strenuous job working my muscles, and I really filled out. Big shoulders and arms, a 16-year-old kid at 300 pounds, stacked like a brick outhouse. That changed the playing field quite a bit for me. Plus, I wound up getting a girlfriend that was like 26 or 27 years old. I was through with high school chicks after that. Everybody else went through that stage where they're pinching butts in the hall and trying to climb up to the window and peek on girls in the shower; I had a girlfriend that drove a Camaro Iroc Z28 with a T-top. She liked me right off the bat, and she took me under her wing. It's funny, but about the first time you get laid is when your confidence starts to come around. From then on, I had so much confi-

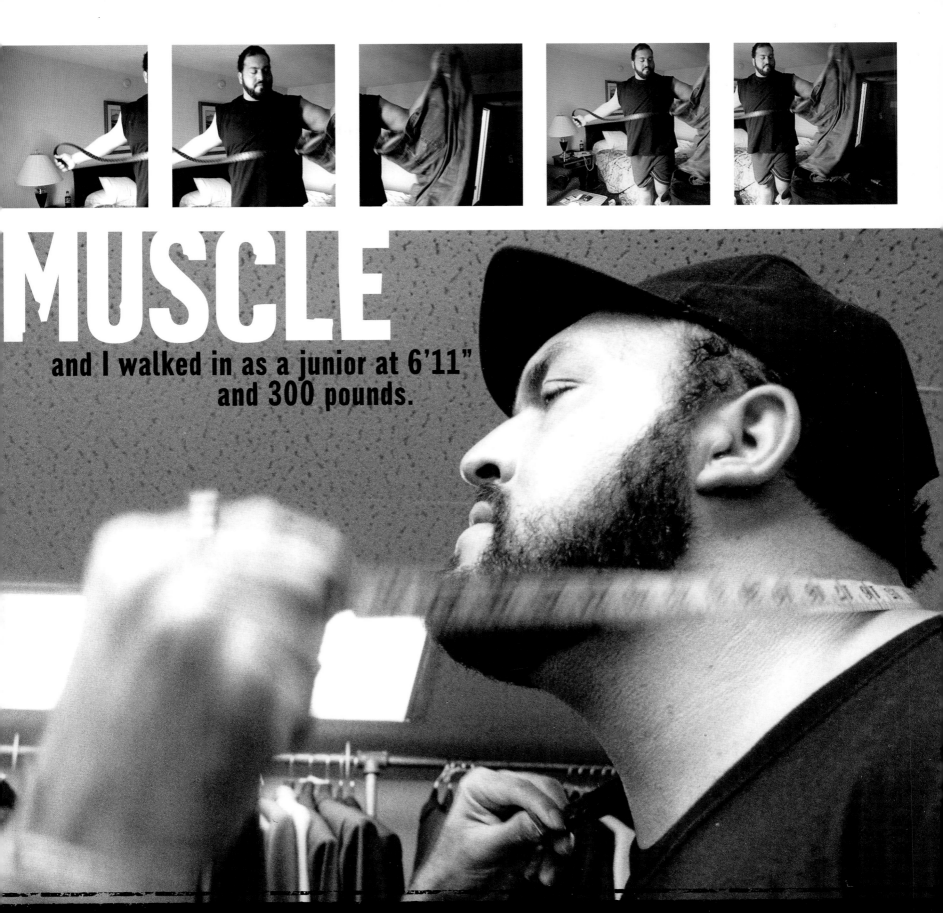

MUSCLE

and I walked in as a junior at 6'11"
and 300 pounds.

dence I became arrogant. At 16 years old, it seemed like everything came together all at once for me, which was a good thing, because it made my social situation at school a lot easier.

I was scoring 45 to 50 points a game in high school. I had one game of 61 points. I was 26 for 27 from the field and 9 for 9 from the free-throw line. I missed one shot all night, and it was a dunk, believe it or not. I went to Northern Oklahoma Junior College for a year, then I signed my letter of intent to Wichita State. The coach I went there for got fired halfway through the season, so I was only there a year. I ran off chasing some girl and wound up going to school at Southern Illinois-Edwardsville, where I hurt my knee, which basically ended basketball for me.

RAP HIT big when I was an early teen, when everybody's a rebel, everybody wants to do something different, go against what your parents say, go against the norm. Right around when Boogie Down Productions was coming out, when NWA was coming out, when the Beasties hit pretty good, that's when I started listening to rap. Here were these guys, these gangstas, these thugs, these guys that could do whatever they want, living the mob lifestyle — I just fell into it. Plus, it was catchy music; you could bob your head to it. I've been messing around with it since I was 15. I went to boarding school when I was 16 — Cushing Academy in Ashburnham, Massachusetts — and one of my buddies who lived on the third floor of my dorm had two turntables and a mic. We'd go up there during study hall, which was two hours a day, put on the turntable and just rhyme. Me and three or four other kids, we'd always be up there, rhyming. It was horrible; we sucked. We tried to be like the people we idolized.

When I got to WWE, I'd rhyme sometimes with some of the guys. One day, the right people overheard it and said, "Hey, we're gonna give that a shot on TV." I was overjoyed. This was something I love to do, and I get to turn the volume way up and be as obnoxious as I want to be. I recently had an open hip-hop challenge to try to get a rapper to come in and battle-rap with me, rap-off with me, just to prove that this isn't a gimmick, that what I'm doing is really me, that I'm not doing it just because they need somebody to do the urban hip-hop gimmick. I challenged a rapper, and none of them showed up. I don't think it's the fact that they're scared, because they're all very talented. I just think it's the fact that I'm a small-town white kid who can actually rhyme a little bit.

I'VE GOT NOTHING TO LOSE.
THEY'VE GOT A LOT TO LOSE IF THEY'RE AN INNER-CITY THUG COMING IN HERE,
AND I MAKE THEM LOOK BAD.

I GREW up in Winnipeg, Canada, and as far back as I can remember I was a big fan of wrestling. I used to watch wrestling on TV all the time. Five o'clock was Roadrunner and Bugs Bunny cartoons. Six o'clock was AWA wrestling. It just started with that, and one day I got to go see a wrestling match live — I think I got tickets for Christmas — and I was into it for good. I remember guys like Nick Bockwinkel, Scott Hall, the High Flyers, Hulk Hogan before he was in the World Wrestling Federation — we're talking the early 1980s. Baron Von Raschke, The Crusher, Sheik Adnan Al Kaissie, Jerry Blackwell — those are the guys I grew up watching.

I'd planned to go to wrestling school since I was 16. I wrote a letter to the Hart brothers pro wrestling camp because they had their address on the Stampede Wrestling show from Calgary that we used to get in Winnipeg. A friend and I had a fantasy that if we hung out around the back door of the wrestling arena, maybe Davey Boy Smith, who was the British Bulldog, and the Dynamite Kid — we were huge fans of theirs — would come out and see us and take us under their wing and make us into the

new British Bulldogs. We used to wait for them all the time. And we'd sneak into the bars and go to the gyms where they went, just try to hang around them. I used to talk to Marty Jannetty and Shawn Michaels, the smaller guys, because they weren't as intimidating as guys like the Warlord, the Barbarian, the Ultimate Warrior, who were just massive.

You had to be 18 to go to wrestling school, and I was only 17 when I graduated from high school. So I went to college, Red River Community College in Winnipeg, and I majored in journalism because it was a two-year program. Sometime in there, I met Jesse "the Body" Ventura at a celebrity hockey game. There was a party afterward, and I had about a two-hour conversation with him. He was really cool, just talking about wrestling. Two things that I remember he said were, one, if you want to be a wrestler be prepared to live each day in pain, which is true. And, number two, make sure you get something you can fall back on. He fell back on being the governor of Minnesota, and I can fall back on being a journalist.

I NEVER DID TALK TO DAVEY OR DYNAMITE. DYNAMITE ALWAYS
LOOKED AT ME VERY EVIL,
LIKE HE WAS GOING TO

BEAT ME UP
IF I SAID ANYTHING TO HIM

I **WAS** out of the big picture for about two and a half years. When I came back, yeah, I was scared. I'm human, man, I always have fear. But I don't believe that a majority of my fear was based on whether the fans were gonna accept me. My biggest fear was about my own inability to perform. I put so much pressure on myself and I put myself to such a high standard that if I don't go out there and be at least semi-perfect, then I'm not happy. I came back for a lot of reasons. It had to do with not being able to watch wrestling on TV without wanting to be a part of it. It had everything to do with being barraged by fan letters and people stopping me on the street and asking me to come back, and saying that they hadn't watched wrestling since I left — that's the biggest honor anyone can be bestowed. Truth be told, I owe a lot to the business, and this is my way of giving back. If it takes going out there and getting my ass slammed around for a couple more years, then so be it. But I plan on being the one doing the slamming.

TRUTH BE TOLD,
I OWE A LOT TO
THE BUSINESS

20

IN CANADA, I had wrestling on TV all weekend. You couldn't get away from wrestling at our house. There was Stampede Wrestling from Calgary, with the British Bulldog, Bret "Hit Man" Hart, Brian Pillman, Owen Hart. Chris Benoit was just starting his career, so I watched him grow up. And we had international wrestling from Montreal. Sweet Daddy Siki wrestled there; that's the guy who ended up training me. Now little kids will come to our front door and give me cookies. You see that smile on their face, they're looking at me the same way I used to look at Hulk Hogan and Bret Hart, and that's pretty cool.

I played hockey from early on, and soccer, baseball, and basketball. But I knew it was wrestling for me. I told my mom that when I was young, and the cool thing about her, through thick and thin, all the way, she always said, "Yeah, go for it, go for it." When I was 17 and still saying it and everyone else was probably snickering behind my back, she was still saying, "Go for it." My mom was married and got pregnant with me — she was 20 — and before I was born, my dad took off. So from day one, it's been her and me.

WRESTLING DREW ME IN AS A KID WHEN I FIRST SAW HULK HOGAN ON TV.
I was 8 or 9, flipping through the channels, and there he was, and I went, "Whoa, what's this? This is so cool." Just so much energy and charisma. I remember thinking, "Wow! The comics I'm reading are real life. I'm reading about Spider-Man and the Incredible Hulk and Thor.
AND THERE'S HULK HOGAN, AND HE'S FLESH AND BLOOD,

and he's LARGER than life."

The Toronto Star ran a wrestling column, and one week there was an item about a contest for free lessons at wrestling school. You needed to write an essay on why you wanted to be a wrestler. Then they submitted the essays to Sully's Gymnasium, to Sweet Daddy Siki and Ron Hutchison. So I wrote my essay, and Sweet Daddy Siki called me and said it was down to me and a few other people, and they wanted me to come in and meet them. I went in, and they chose me, and that was the beginning. I was 17 years old, 6'2" or 6'3", about 180 pounds. I guess they saw what I could mature into, thankfully. I was tall and had shoulders; there was just no muscle on the shoulders yet.

I wish I had kept a copy of the essay. I just remember not trying to embarrass myself. I knew enough at that point not to make a complete idiot of myself, not to say, "I'm a huge *Hulkamaniac*, yada, yada, yada." I knew enough to say, "I realize I'm probably not going to make money at first, if ever, but this is truly what I want to do." When they met me, they told me, "We have eaten out of dumpsters, we have struggled to get by. Do you want to do this?" I didn't even hesitate. I went, "Hell, yeah."

MY BROTHER Jeff and I both live just outside of Cameron, North Carolina, which has about 300 people. We were born and raised here on a farm in the woods. We had tobacco barns, and my dad was a rural mail carrier. Coming from such a humble background, after we got to the WWE and became established, I'm sure we both asked ourselves if we should live someplace else where there was more glamour and glitz — but neither one of us was ever serious about leaving. After going to New York City a couple of times, you'd have to pay me to live there. I see plenty of

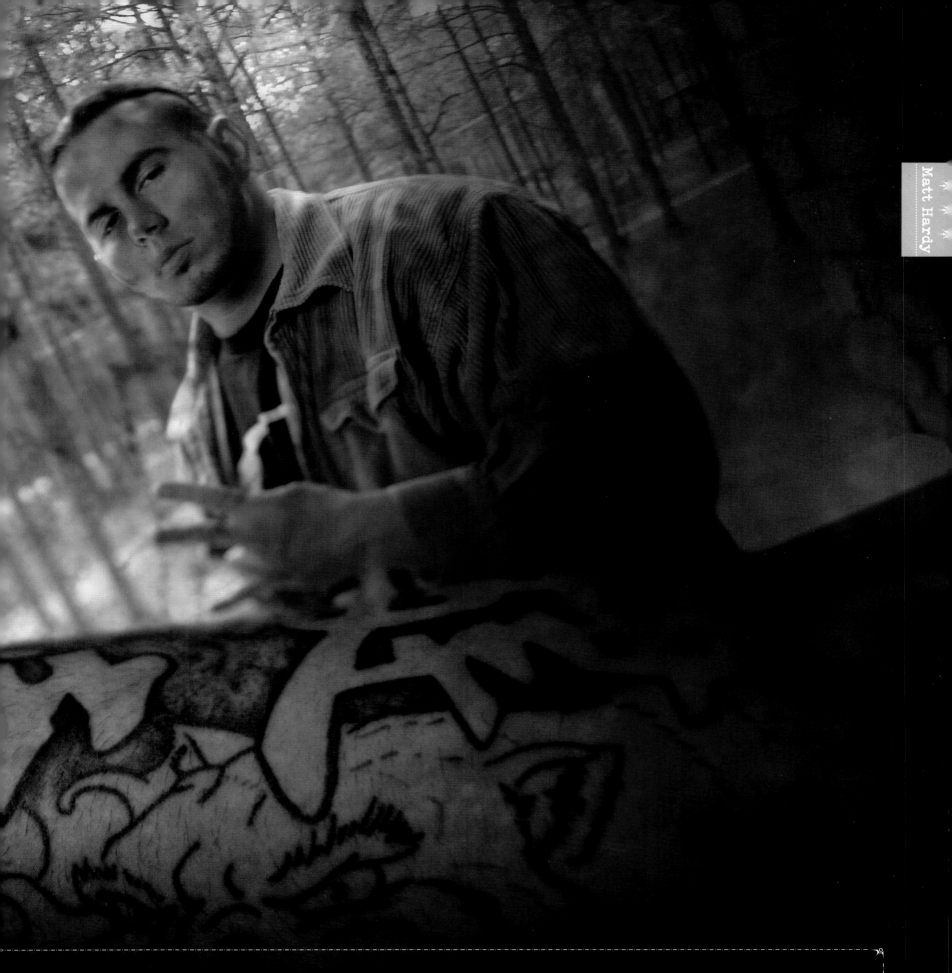

glamour and glitz, as it is. It's nice to be able to get away from that and come back here and walk down the streets of Cameron and talk to people you've known all your life, and just keep your head level. Being out here in the country and having acres of land, you can go outside naked if you want. It's great to have that freedom, to play music as loud as you want, to scream as loud as you want. I just love it here, man. It's my element; it's a part of my heart.

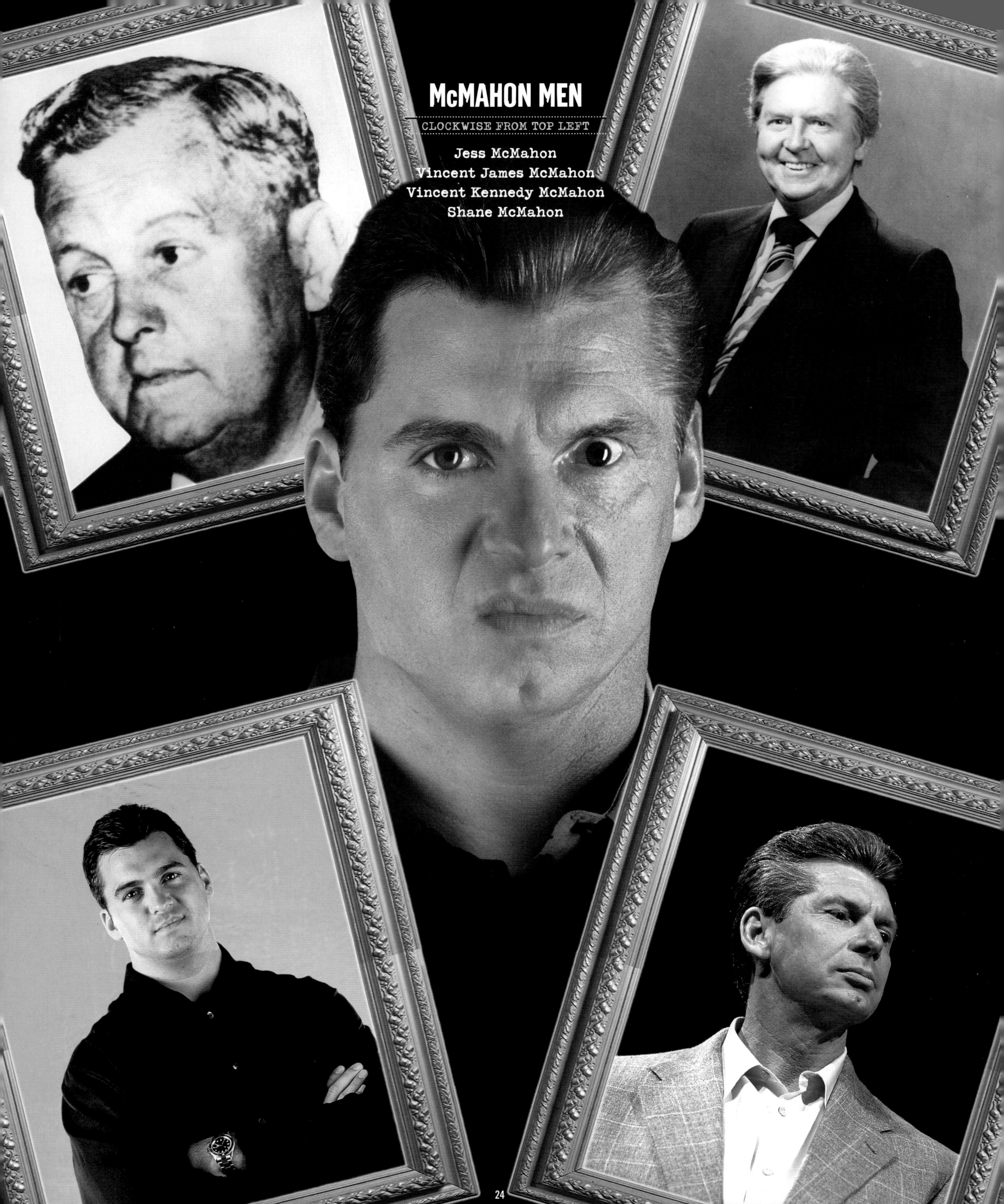

McMAHON MEN

CLOCKWISE FROM TOP LEFT

Jess McMahon
Vincent James McMahon
Vincent Kennedy McMahon
Shane McMahon

24

I am **very** proud to carry the name McMahon and be the fourth generation in the promotions business. My great-grandfather Jess McMahon promoted boxing and wrestling for Tex Rickart at Madison Square Garden back in the early 1900's. His son, my grandfather, Vincent J. McMahon followed in this tradition and founded and grew what was then known as the "northeast territory", stemming from Washington D.C. to Maine. Madison Square Garden was and is considered to be home to our family's business. This "territory" was then known as The World Wrestling Federation. During this time my grandfather discovered the talents of Andre the Giant, Bruno Sammartino, Pedro Morales, Freddie Blassie, Gorilla Monsoon and even a young unknown, who would later become Hulk Hogan.

My father, Vincent K. McMahon was first introduced to his dad's business as a teenager and fell in love with it immediately. After working many years with his father, my dad took over and turned the wrestling business on its ear and changed its landscape forever. In 1985, Madison Square Garden, became home to the biggest event of them all; the first ever *WrestleMania.*

Unlike my dad, my introduction to the business happened at a much earlier age, but its impact on me was the same. I was just a little boy when I fell in love with the larger than life characters, the athleticism and the storylines. I remember standing backstage watching my dad and being so proud to be his son. I wanted to grow up and be just like him. As a man, I realize how lucky I am to be able to follow in the footsteps of three generations of extraordinary McMahon men. I hope that in my lifetime, I can make the kind of contributions they made to this business, and that they will be as proud of me, as I have been to carry on their name.

I HAD always wanted to pursue acting, so I moved to LA and started taking acting classes three or four times a week. A friend of mine in LA, Rich Minzer, knows a lot of the wrestlers, and he took me to a WCW show. I had never watched wrestling before; we didn't have cable when I was growing up. We got backstage, and I met Kevin Nash, and Kevin asked if I'd be interested in doing a little thing with a guy they wanted to bring in, David Flair. It was only supposed to last a few months, but it worked out really well, and I stuck around.

At first, I was just a valet going to the ring with somebody, but I've become a wrestler. It's crazy, because when I got into wrestling, if you had told me I was going to be a wrestler, I never would have believed it. But you almost can't be a girl in wrestling these days without wrestling; people love seeing us mix it up. And it's so much more fun to be able to get in there and mix it up instead of just standing around on the side of the ring.

For me, wrestling is the perfect combination of the two loves of my life. I love to perform, and I love being athletic. The two together are a perfect mix for me.

I COMPETED IN FITNESS COMPETITIONS AND DID A LOT OF FITNESS MODELING WHILE I WAS STILL IN IDAHO, WHICH IS WHERE I GREW UP.

Torrie Wilson
TORRIE GRUNER

AFTER DOING THAT A FEW YEARS, IT KIND OF GAVE ME THE GUTS TO TRY MY LUCK IN LOS ANGELES.

I was into wrestling as a child, probably from about the time I was 3. I would always watch it on TV, but I would only watch what at the time was World Wrestling Federation. I never watched any of the other promotions because I knew they were competition. I was always very proud of my family and what we did.

I ACTUALLY KICKED A BOY IN THE SHINS IN SECOND GRADE FOR MAKING FUN OF MY FATHER.

I'M THE vice president of television writing, which means I manage the writing team, of which my dad is the head. I help work on both shows. There's a separate writing team for *Raw* and for *SmackDown!* I help write both. On Mondays, I'm producing and directing. On Tuesdays, I'm part of the show, and sometimes I'm producing and directing, too. I started working for the company when I was about 12, interning in different positions. I worked the switchboard for a couple of years, and to this day I remember the extensions — I used to have dreams about those extensions. I also worked in human resources, media relations, marketing, live events, promotion, Pay-Per-View promotion, new media — the Internet — and as a production assistant in the television studio. After I graduat-ed college, I had two really unique internships. I interned with my mother, who's the company CEO, for about three months. I got to sit in on every meeting, listen to every phone call that was business-related, read everything that came across her desk, and I got to ask questions about all of it. Then I spent six months with my father. Again, I was in every meeting, on every phone call — I learned the cre-ative side of the business that way, and I just fell in love with it. No where else can you do all the things that I love to do, which is write, perform, direct, pro-duce, and be involved in marketing and promotion. To work alongside my family and to be able to be a part of the business that I love — it's the best to me. It is work a lot of times, but I love to do it. I have a passion for it.

Stephanie McMahon

I HAVE A BACHELOR'S DEGREE IN ENGLISH,

AND I THOUGHT THAT I WANTED TO TEACH. I DID SOME SUBSTITUTE TEACHING IN JUNIOR HIGH SCHOOL IN THE ST. LOUIS AREA, AND THE BATTLES I FIGHT HERE ARE NOTHING COMPARED TO THE BATTLES THAT YOU FIGHT THERE.

AFTER DOING THAT, TEACHERS HAVE MY RESPECT; THAT'S A PRETTY HARD PROFESSION. I'VE GOT A PHYSICAL PRESENCE AND I COULD GET THE KIDS' ATTENTION, BUT IT'S JUST CHANGED SO MUCH SINCE I WAS A KID. BACK THEN, WE SHOWED RESPECT TO OUR TEACHERS. AND UNFORTUNATELY, IN A LOT OF SITUATIONS NOW,

TEACHERS DON'T HAVE THE SUPPORT OF THE PARENTS THAT THEY NEED.
SO IF I WASN'T DOING THIS, I DON'T THINK I'D BE TEACHING.

Vince McMahon gets a kick out of my colloquiums, my being a redneck from Oklahoma.

Contrary to what people may perceive,

VINCE IS A NORTH CAROLINA REDNECK.

HE WAS RAISED IN AN EIGHT-FOOT WIDE TRAILER, HIS MOM HAD MULTIPLE HUSBANDS, AND THE MAJORITY OF THEM USED TO BEAT THE HELL OUT OF VINCE WITH WRENCHES AND TOOLS AND BELTS AND THEIR FISTS. HE HAD A VERY CHALLENGING UPBRINGING. HE'S THE ONLY PERSON I'VE EVER MET THAT WAS COURT-MARTIALED IN MILITARY SCHOOL AS A KID. HE HAD WWE "ATTITUDE" BEFORE THERE WAS A WWE. HE HAD TO FIGHT HIS ASS OFF TO GET INTO THE BUSINESS. HIS DAD DIDN'T WANT VINCE IN THE BUSINESS, PERIOD, END OF DISCUSSION. HIS DAD MADE IT VERY DIFFICULT FOR VINCE TO BUY THE COMPANY. VINCE DIDN'T INHERIT ANYTHING; HE BOUGHT THE COMPANY WITH BORROWED MONEY, LEVERAGED MONEY, ROBBING PETER TO PAY PAUL — COMPLETELY A RIVERBOAT GAMBLER AND ENTREPRENEURIAL MENTALITY. HE HAD A VISION FOR GROWTH AND WHERE THE BUSINESS WAS GONNA BE. I WENT TO A MEETING IN KANSAS CITY ONE TIME WHERE A BUNCH OF PROMOTERS WERE TALKING ABOUT HOW TO COMBAT THIS UPSTART KID NAMED VINCE MCMAHON. I WAS SITTING ON THE THRONE, IN THE BATHROOM WHEN TWO OR THREE OLD PROMOTERS CAME IN AND TALKED ABOUT KILLING HIM. ONE OF THEM SAID, "I DON'T KNOW WHY WE'RE HAVING THIS FUCKING MEETING. I GOT BETTER THINGS TO DO; YOU GOT BETTER THINGS TO DO, LET'S JUST HAVE THE SUMBITCH KILLED." I'M SITTING THERE AND I WANT TO PULL MY FEET UP ABOVE THE DOOR; I DON'T WANT TO BE AN ACCOMPLICE TO THIS CRAP. MY BOSS AT THE TIME, COWBOY BILL WATTS, WAS ONE OF THE THREE, AND HE TOLD ME, "THAT'S JUST THOSE OLD-TIMERS BLOWING OFF STEAM. THEY'RE NOT GONNA KILL NOTHING BUT TIME." HE SAID, "THEY'VE GOTTEN LAZY, THEY'VE GOTTEN COMPLACENT, AND THEY'VE FORGOTTEN HOW TO PROMOTE. THIS GUY'S HUNGRY, HE'S AGGRESSIVE, AND HE KNOWS HOW TO PROMOTE."

THE ONLY WRESTLING I GOT TO WATCH
AS A KID WAS AT MY COUSINS' HOUSE.
IT WASN'T ALLOWED AT MY HOUSE.
MY MOM'S QUOTE WAS,

"WRESTLING CAUSES BRAIN DAMAGE."

SHE THOUGHT IT MADE YOU STUPID; I THINK SHE'S WRONG.

AT MY cousins' house, after we watched, they'd take me in the basement and do all the moves on me and beat me up. I didn't know how to defend myself, because I didn't watch very often. So I'd get elbow drop after elbow drop off the couch, and I'd just have to take it. My senior year at Harvard, I lived with five of my football teammates in a two-bedroom apartment off campus that had cable TV. They were all wrestling fans, and we had one television and one couch, so every Monday and Thursday night we all hung out together and watched wrestling. That's when I started loving it; it's so easy to get into it.

When you've got a degree from Harvard and you want to be a professional wrestler, yes, it is difficult to approach your parents and tell them what you want to do. But it's easier to tell them when you're not asking for money. I still had a consulting job, which I was working part-time, so it was like, "I'm still going to pay my bills; I'm still going to support myself; but I'm also going to be pursuing this wrestling thing." They really couldn't say anything; they couldn't cut me off or anything. They at first thought I was really weird and thought I might have taken too many head shots playing football. But they started watching wrestling to get into it, and they started to appreciate the skill and the artistry about it. They understood how I could fall in love with it.

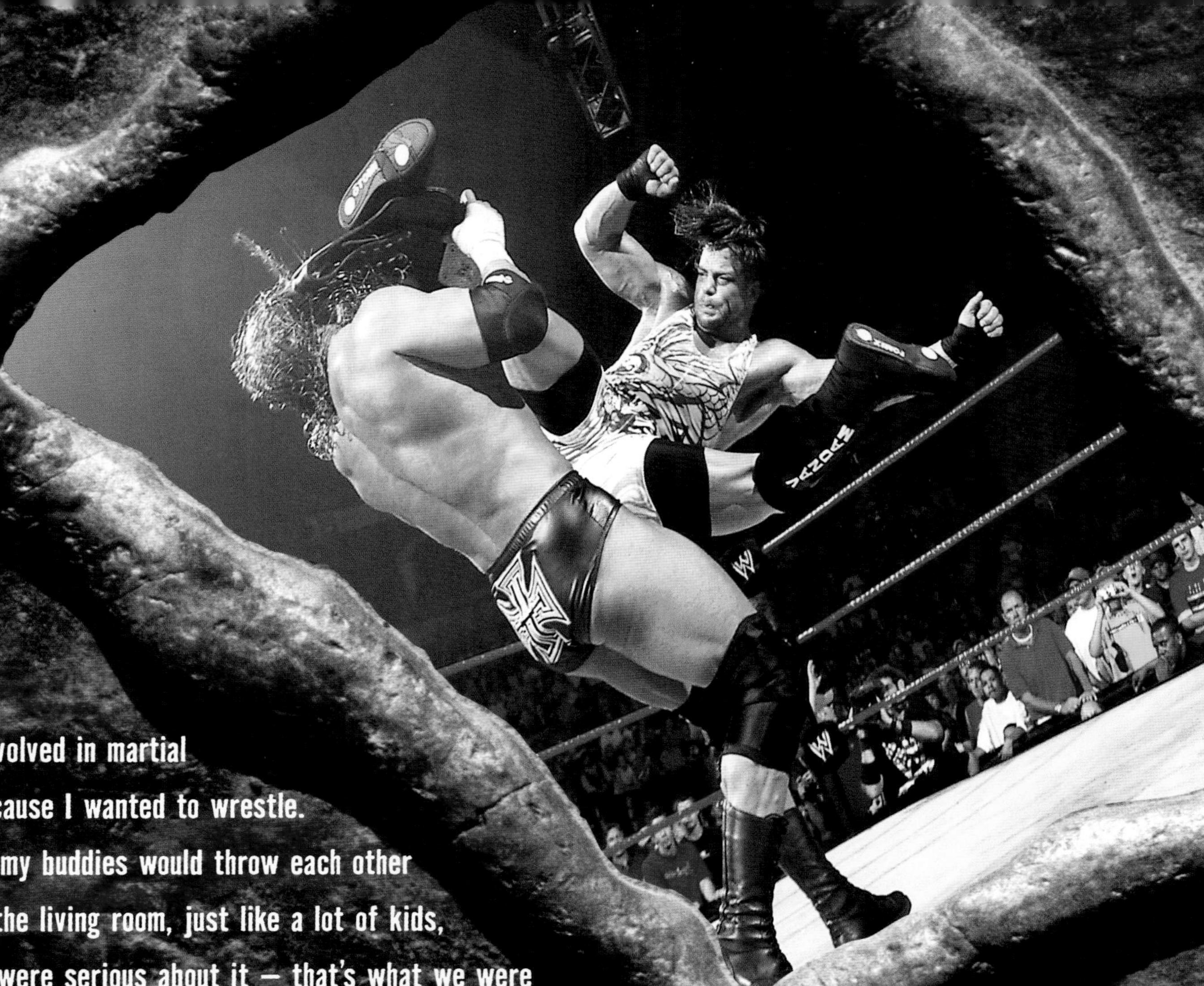

I got involved in martial

arts because I wanted to wrestle.

Me and my buddies would throw each other

around the living room, just like a lot of kids,

but we were serious about it — that's what we were

going to do when we grew up. We found out that a guy in

our town—Battle Creek—Michigan, had a ring in his yard,

so we went to talk to him, and it turned out that

he was a kickboxing promoter. He said,

"Show up, and I'll let you guys

work out."

We had to go through his stretches, his kickboxing classes, sparring with his students, kicking his bag, all the drills — and after all that crap, when the kickboxers would go home, then the wrestlers could have the ring. That's how I got into martial arts, but it turned out that I really liked it. I trained with several dojos around Battle Creek and even continued after I started my career in wrestling and was moving from state to state.

I STARTED training at this gym between my junior and senior years of college,
and I met a guy there who was trying to find somebody
to go to wrestling school with him. I was interested, but I had basketball.
I went to college on a basketball scholarship, and I was
good enough that I was getting offers to go overseas and play professionally.
People I talked to that knew wrestling said,

"YOU FILL OUT A LITTLE BIT, AT 6'8",

YOU COULD GO SOMEPLACE."

I was a fan of wrestling, but I had put all this time into basketball. But the reality hit me one day:
At best, I was gonna have two or three years in pro basketball, probably in Italy or some other place overseas
I didn't want to be. So I decided to give wrestling a chance. I upset a lot of people when
I left college; I was 10 credits short of my degree. But I had realized
at that point what I wanted to do, and the opportunity was there, and I wanted to seize that opportunity.

MY OLDEST BROTHER TOLD ME,
"LOOK, MARK, YOU DON'T LIVE YOUR LIFE FOR EVERYBODY ELSE.
YOU HAVE TO DO WHAT'S RIGHT FOR YOU. YOU CAN'T WORRY ABOUT
WHAT MOM AND DAD THINK, OR YOUR COACH THINKS.
YOU AIN'T HURTING ANYBODY ELSE. YOU'RE GONNA LIVE,
YOU'RE GONNA SURVIVE BY YOUR OWN ACTIONS."
THAT WAS PRETTY MUCH ALL I NEEDED TO HEAR.
I TOOK IT FROM THERE.

Once I was working every week, I knew that I would make it. Did I know that I would make it
to the level that I did? No; you can't foresee anything like that. There for a while, I lived in my car.
Pretty much all my money went to food. But I wasn't going to ask anybody for help,
I had too much pride. And I didn't want to hear any flak about not finishing college.
Not that I'm proud I didn't get my degree, but I had made my choice.

I THINK the people took to me because I'm basically just like everybody else. My favorite place to shop is Wal-Mart; you get the Wal-Mart crowd, you pretty much got everybody. Doing the anti-authority thing, going against your boss — that appeals to blue-collar, white-collar, everybody.

When you look at the people we're trying to cater to, look at it like a whole pie, and the slices are all the demographics. Well, I'm covering everybody from kids to teenagers to middle-aged people to old people, and even girls, for whatever reason that is. Some of the wrestlers are too good-looking, so the girlfriends automatically like them and their boyfriends hate them just for that fact that they're good-looking. I don't try to cater to that crowd, but nonetheless I end up getting them, just for who I am. So that means I've got all the pieces of the pie covered — that's what I believe. I do have a small section of people who think the "Austin 3:16" thing is sacrilegious, so they get mad at me. Hey, that's good, because when you've got a few people throwing rocks at you, that makes people who like you stand up for you all that much more.

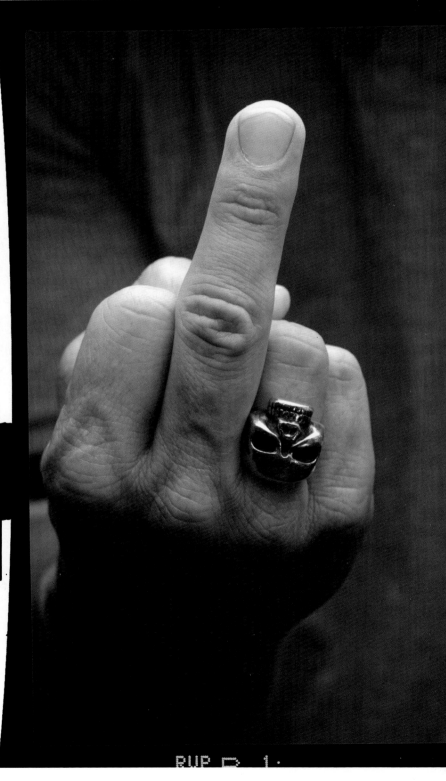

WHAT YOU SEE OF ME ON TV AND ME IN REAL LIFE IS PRETTY MUCH THE SAME GUY. I'M JUST SOME GUY THAT'S NOT AFRAID TO SAY

"SCREW YOU, RAISE HELL, DRINK BEER, FLIP PEOPLE OFF." I'M NOT CUSSING' RIGHT NOW, BUT

I started off in the business as Steve Williams, then a guy gave me the name Steve Austin, and then he gave me "Stunning" Steve Austin. I was searching for what my character was supposed to be. When I came up to WWE, they originally started calling me the Ringmaster — I knew that sucked. They started to give me some interview time, and Vince McMahon was editing the lines that I was saying. So I told him, "Vince, you got guys here that are 6'10", 7 feet; 300, 350 pounds. I'm 6'2", 250 pounds; I wear black boots, black trunks; I got a bald head and a goatee. If you take my personality away from me, I can't compete with anybody here. But if you give me my personality, I can compete with anybody. Hell, without a personality, what am I? Nothing."

Vince listened to me, and he stopped chopping all my lines up. Somewhere around that time I watched a TV special on Richard Kuklinski, the serial killer, and that's where I got the idea for my character. After I watched that show on Kuklinski, we came up with Stone Cold Steve Austin, this hell-raisin', beer-drinkin' machine who flips people off and doesn't really give a damn. Then all I did was just basically be myself. In a million years, I didn't think it was gonna turn into what it did.

RVP

CBCCAF-AGEC

RVP ▷ 2.

I PRETTY MUCH CUSS LIKE A SAILOR, 24-7.

IF YOU HUNG AROUND WITH ME FOR ABOUT A WEEK, YOU'D FIND OUT THAT EVERY BIT OF THAT IS TRUE. AND YOU'D HAVE A PRETTY GOOD GUT TO GO ALONG WITH IT, TOO.

I **NEVER** lived in the same house with my dad. I was very independent and grew up pretty much on the street, much to my mom's chagrin. But she couldn't control me. It was a crazy environment that I grew up in. When you're a kid and you get the crap beat out of you by your stepfathers — that's no fun. But all that really worked to my advantage, because it made me tougher, without losing a degree of sensitivity. Had I not had that background, I probably wouldn't have been able to deal with these tough-guy wrestling promoters that were threatening me when I was going into other territories and expanding the company. I'm truculent by nature, love to fight, and always did as a kid. I wasn't what people who knew my dad would expect. My dad was a really classy guy; he should have been canonized. I was different from my father in a lot of respects — far more aggressive, more physical, and more demonstrative in every way. If I like you, I'm going to tell you. I'm a hugger, even with men; I'm just very visceral.

I WAS LOOKED UPON AS THIS 800-POUND GORILLA, GOBBLING UP ALL THESE LITTLE TERRITORIES.

BUT I WAS THE 120-POUND CHIMPANZEE WITH A SET OF NUTS AS BIG AS THE GORILLA'S.

THAT'S ALL I HAD — A BLUFF, AND A VERY, VERY STRONG WORK ETHIC. ALL THESE PROMOTERS INDIVIDUALLY HAD
FAR MORE RESOURCES THAN I DID, FROM A MONETARY STANDPOINT; THEY JUST DIDN'T HAVE THE CHUTZPAH TO GO WITH IT.

HISPANIC WRESTLERS have been wearing masks since way back.

ONE OF the top wrestling superstars of all time in Mexico was El Santo. He used to wear a silver mask, and he had these awesome matches, advanced for his time. The fans were so into the character with the silver mask and the silver tights. El Santo would never show his face; he would do interviews for television, and he would be in the mask. So a lot of wrestlers started to come out with masks. It got to a point where they would have a mask-versus-mask match, and the loser would have to take off his mask. Maybe you would be following this wrestler for 10, 15 years, and you never knew who he was, so you'd say, "I'm going to pay for a ticket to go see who's gonna lose. I'm gonna see his face for the first time." The vendors would go out among the fans, and they would sell masks of the wrestlers. Little kids would pick out whoever their favorite superstar was and put his mask on, and the TV camera would come by, and you would see the little kid in the mask, cheering and happy. It brought out a lot of emotion for the fans.

WRESTLING WAS my first love, but my first plan was to be the first one from my family to go to college and graduate. But for a long time growing up, I didn't have any plan at all. When I was 13, 14, 15, 16, I got into so much trouble. I had been arrested 5 or 6 times by the time I was 16 for fighting, theft, you name it. I knew I had to change my life and stop fucking up — excuse my language — or else who knows what would have happened to me, especially with the people I was running with. I started playing football and fell in love with the game, which opened up a lot of doors and opportunities. I got scholarship offers and went to the University of Miami and played football. As things happened, that chapter of my life closed. I had always known that I wanted one day to become a wrestler and so I decided now was the time to take a swing at it. My dad was adamantly against me getting in the business. He had come up in the business at a different time and it was hard, especially for a man of color. He was very successful at what he did; he became the first Black champion in many promotions across the country. But we didn't have much at all; we had a lot of nothing, basically — and my dad didn't want that for his son, naturally.

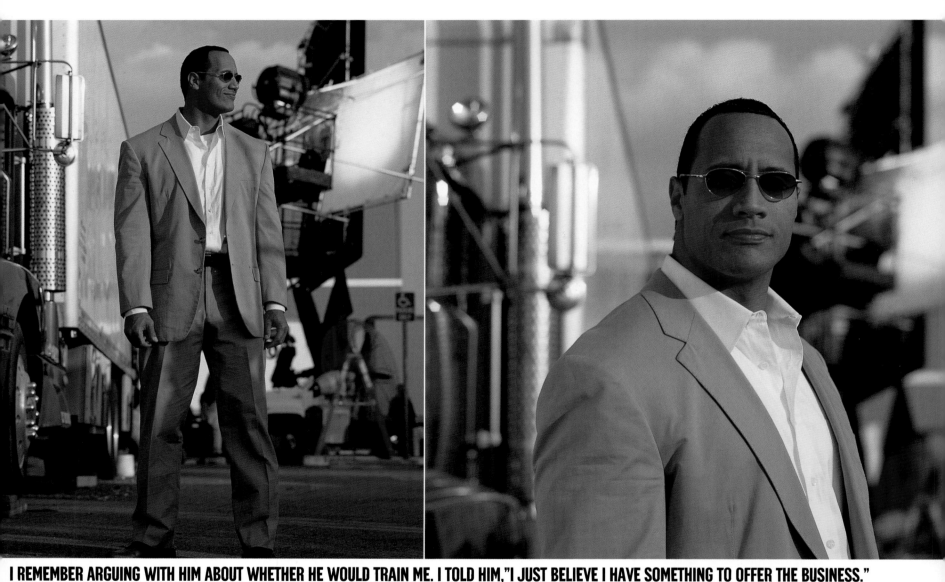

I REMEMBER ARGUING WITH HIM ABOUT WHETHER HE WOULD TRAIN ME. I TOLD HIM,"I JUST BELIEVE I HAVE SOMETHING TO OFFER THE BUSINESS."
AND HE CAME AT ME WITH,
"WELL, WHAT IS IT YOU HAVE TO OFFER?"
ALL I COULD COME UP WITH WAS,
"FUCK IF I KNOW."

MY TATTOO is the story of my life symbolically in Polynesian and Samoan artwork. Tattoos in the Samoan customs are very meaningful. My grandfather, who was the paramount high chief in Samoa, had a tattoo that was basically the same design as mine, very similar in tone, the same color, very dark, very heavy-handed. His started at his knees and went all the way around his legs and up across his groin and around his butt and all the way up to right below his chest. Mine was done by a friend who only does spiritual tattoos and Polynesian tattoos. It took 35 hours, and I had it done over two days. There was an extreme amount of pain involved because he had to be heavy-handed to get the color as dark as it needed to be and because of all the territory he had to cover; mine crosses a lot of my arm, my shoulder, my back, and into my chest. By that 17th hour each day, the pain was excruciating. By that time, my body was completely spent up and had released every endorphin to combat the pain that it possibly could.

I GOT into wrestling in 1972 when I was 22. Before that, I was selling life insurance, and my wife — my first wife — was a dental assistant. A friend of mine who was a life insurance agent brought it to my attention that if I got my life insurance license, I could go around and sell to all my friends and make some good money for a couple of years. We were doing OK. I probably made $50,000 that first year selling life insurance and I had a new Buick Riviera. But it wasn't like I was a successful businessman. I was making a living because I had a lot of friends; I was selling life insurance to first-time customers with the help of an agent. I just brought them in; he wrote the contracts. I got bored with it, and I was running out of friends to sell to. The wrestling thing came around because I knew a guy by the name of Ken Patera, who was a 1972 Olympian in weightlifting. He had moved to Minneapolis and was being sponsored for the Olympics by Verne Gagne, who owned the AWA. Verne was going to break Ken into the business after Ken came back from Munich. I was lucky enough to be with Ken, and off we went. My mom and dad were pretty successful — my dad was a doctor and my mom was the assistant director of the Tyrone Guthrie Theater in Minneapolis.

WHEN I TOLD THEM I WAS GOING INTO WRESTLING, WELL, I'LL PUT IT LIKE THIS: THEY WEREN'T OVER THE TOP ON THE IDEA.

Some weeks, I'd make $200; some weeks I'd make $300 or $400. I was clearly spending more than I was making. I was struggling big-time, but I was enjoying it, so I didn't look at it as struggling. I was with a lot of great people, guys that I just idolized once I got in the business and got to know them. Dusty Rhodes, Wahoo McDaniel, Ray Stevens, Nick Bockwinkel, Dick Murdoch, Larry Hennig, Harley Race, the creame d' creame back then.

I DON'T KNOW WHAT I WOULD HAVE DONE IF I HADN'T GOTTEN INTO WRESTLING, BUT I ALWAYS FELT LIKE I WAS GONNA BE SUCCESSFUL .

I DON'T KNOW IF I WOULD HAVE BEEN FAMOUS OR NOT, BUT I ALWAYS I THOUGHT I WAS GONNA DO SOMETHING. BOOKWISE, I WASN'T THE SMARTEST KID IN THE WORLD, BUT I KNEW THAT I WASN'T GOING TO BE ONE OF THOSE KIDS WHO DIDN'T SEE LIFE, WHO DIDN'T EXPERIENCE LIFE AND DO WHAT HE WANTED TO DO.

I had a very good childhood, I think. In actuality, you don't know what you've got and what you don't have if you've never had it before. We felt like we had everything we needed. My father died when I was 10 months old, and my mother raised all of us — there were four boys and four girls — until she died when I was about 14. I played sports around the neighborhood, but I never played any organized sports in school. Dancing was my outlet; that and being free, being my own person. I was an outcast pretty much, because I was just totally different than most kids. I would spend a day with a screwdriver poking holes in my jeans and then washing them three or four times to make the fringe come out of them so I could walk around with holey jeans before everybody was wearing holey jeans. I cut up my shirts and put them back together with safety pins. It was just being different, I guess.

I've pretty much done things my way since I was 16. Back then, I rebelled, didn't want to listen to anyone. When you're a kid, you don't always understand how much trouble you can get into for doing something wrong. Peer pressure is a big thing also, having friends that urge you to do something that normally you wouldn't. I got myself into a situation where I was an accessory to a crime, a robbery, and I went to prison for almost two years. I easily could have blamed somebody, and came out and did the same thing and ended up back in, which statistics said probably would happen — the rate of a person going out and coming back in is like 60 percent. You have to want to make a change, and I knew there was something better in life for me. When I walked out, I knew I wanted to start fresh, get my life back on track. There were certain things I had to do, as far as getting myself situated in a home environment, and that's where my brother came in and kinda got me on the right track, pulled me under his wing. From that point on, it was gravy.

I GOT in it in 1985, when it was still a territorial business and the money wasn't nearly what it can be today. For me, it had nothing to do with money. From the time I was 12, when I first saw wrestling, I never thought about any other form of life's work for me. I graduated high school and told my dad that I wanted to try wrestling. He got me in touch with a local promoter. We talked, and both of them said, "Get a college education so you have something to fall back on." I went to two semesters at Southwest Texas State and had a 1.4 GPA. I was put on academic probation and, in so many words, asked not to come back for a while. I told my dad at that point, "I'm only going to waste your money; I don't have any desire for school." All I thought about was wrestling. I was studying speech communications because I figured that would help me when I was doing interviews and promos as a wrestler.

I wasn't on the fast track. I started in wrestling by getting beat up every night in the first match on the card. Slowly, as I moved from territory to territory, I went up a little bit higher on the card. My first week, I think I made 700 bucks. I wrestled seven days for it, and because I was traveling every day, I spent probably most of it on the road. But still I thought, "700 bucks! Wow! This is fantastic."

I made enough money to live and eat and have a studio apartment — I was 19, 20 years old and didn't need any more than that. I even saved a little money; I've never been somebody who had the ability to spend more than I had or more than I made. I was doing OK, and I was having a fantastic time.

At first, I was quiet, intimidated, nervous, shy — all the stuff that I really was in real life when I got into wrestling. Then about two years into it, when I went to Minnesota, I became part of a tag team with Marty Jannetty; we were the Midnight Rockers. Marty brought me out of my shell. We enjoyed some success there, and that's when I really became a wrestler 100 percent of the time — the lifestyle, everything. We'd be up all night running around, and we'd go out and wrestle 20 or 30 minutes, and we'd do the same thing all over again the next day. I lived that way for the better part of 15 years. I really have no idea as I look back now how I did it all those years and was able to stay healthy and perform well. I guess it's youth — and ignorance. I know it's a lot of ignorance, not knowing that your body is probably screaming in pain. I've seen other guys do it, too, maybe for longer than I did. There's an old saying, "Wrestlers are a different breed of person," and I think to an extent that's probably true.

I take a lot of pride in that I'm one of the last guys that had hands-on training from Stu Hart when I went to the Hart Family to train. Stu was in his 60s when I went through, but he made me scream and yell. I'd get out of high school on Friday, take the Greyhound bus down to Calgary, which was 180 miles south of where I lived, and stay at the Hart house for the weekend. During the day, I'd work out with Bruce Hart, Mr. Hito, and Mike Hammer. After that, Stu would come out and do a few things in the ring with me, then take me downstairs to the "Dungeon" and stretch me out a bit. It was a good experience just to be there, to imagine all the people that had been through there, and all the blood, sweat and tears that had been paid.

GOING TO THE HART FAMILY FOR TRAINING WAS KIND OF LIKE,

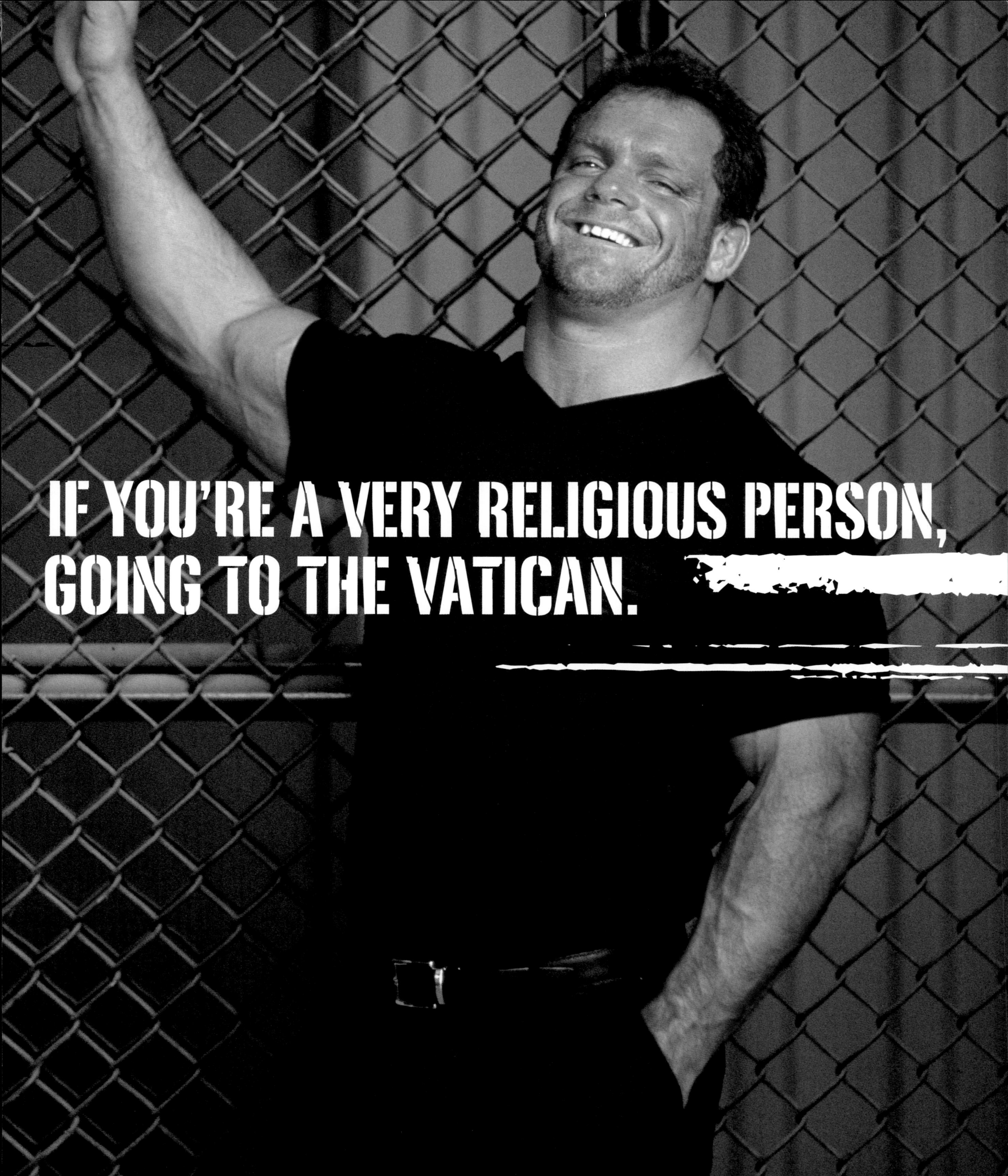

IF YOU'RE A VERY RELIGIOUS PERSON, GOING TO THE VATICAN.

IT WAS THE *TOUGH ENOUGH* PROGRAM THAT GAVE ME THE OPPORTUNITY TO BE WHERE I'M AT TODAY. I'VE ALWAYS, ALWAYS BEEN A HUGE FAN OF WRESTLING. MY FATHER TOOK ME TO MY FIRST MATCH WHEN I WAS ABOUT SEVEN YEARS OLD, AND FROM THEN ON I'VE BEEN AMAZED WITH THE ATHLETICISM, AND INTELLIGENCE THAT GOES ON IN THAT RING.

FOR A kid growing up, wrestlers are the closest thing to real-life super-heroes. But I never once dreamed in any way that this was a career possibility. If you had asked me, "How do you become a professional wrestler?" that would have been like asking me, "How do you become an astronaut?" I didn't have a clue. But I kept up my interest in wrestling as I got older, and I was still following it after college. One day, I was watching *Raw* and I heard Jim Ross say, "Have you ever wanted to become a WWE Superstar?" And I said outloud, "Oh yeah, of course!" With a competition like *Tough Enough*, you can't go into it thinking you have a chance. I sent a tape in — I don't even know if I was being serious when I sent it — but I figured, "Why not?" They wanted just three minutes on tape; they wanted to see your look, your build, and your personality as a character. About a week and a half later, I got a call. I thought it was one of my roommates ribbing me; I thought he was

having some girl call. She said, "This is Carrie from MTV and WWE's *Tough Enough*." And I was like, "Yeah, whatever." And — click! — I hung up. Luckily, she called back. So I called my friend and said, "Did you set this up?" And he said, "No. Not at all." So I realized it wasn't a joke. I got all my stuff together, still thinking, "I'll go to New York, have a chance to meet some of my idols, meet some of the guys I watch every week, just have a good time with it" — thinking there was absolutely no chance to possibly even get picked to be in the house. One thing led to another there, and I was picked to be in the house. So then I went to the house thinking, "This will be an opportunity to get some training, get a little bit of TV exposure, but realistically, what are the odds they're gonna pick me?" It's been out of my hands; it's been at a higher power.

MY LIFE HAS NOT BEEN THE SAME SINCE, IN ANY STRETCH OF THE IMAGINATION. ABSOLUTELY NO PORTION OF MY LIFE HAS BEEN THE SAME SINCE.

I'D SAY I'm pretty into music. I've played and sung, off and on. I wouldn't consider myself good or great by any means; I do it strictly for enjoyment. As I'm getting older, I've broadened to where I can pretty much find enjoyment in almost any kind of music. But growing up, I was strictly, strictly punk rock. There's a huge gap in pop culture for me from the time I was 15 to 22 or 23. Somebody can say, "Do you know this song?" and if it's not punk rock, I'll go, "Never heard it in my life." It could have been a number one hit, but in those years I was just into collecting records and listening to my punk rock, and I never flipped on the radio.

The tattoo on my neck I got just because I had just turned 18 and I was finally allowed to get a tattoo. It says "Rebel" in Russian. I didn't want it in English because I didn't want people that were walking down the street to be able to read it. And I didn't want one with Asian lettering because they were really popular at the time. So I picked this one. I tell everybody it means "Rebel," but it actually means "Iconoclast," which is a form of a rebel. But rather than having to explain to people what "Iconoclast" means, I just give them my abbreviated answer.

The tattoo on my shoulder I got as a souvenir traveling around Europe, at a pit stop in Amsterdam. I was familiar with the artist, knew he was a good artist, and trusted him. I showed him some stuff out of a book, as far as the style that I liked, and I said, "You do whatever you want to do, I trust you. I just want to be able to wear a short-sleeve shirt, have at it." I figured with him being a good artist and me giving him some freedom, it could only turn out that much better. I like it, it's fine. As big as it is, people are kind of shocked that it doesn't have a really deep meaning behind it, other than that I've always been independent and spontaneous, and it's kind of the antithesis of that.

THE TATTOO ON THE INSIDE OF MY LIP I GOT WHEN I WAS LIVING IN A GROUP HOUSE WITH ABOUT 10 PEOPLE, INCLUDING A BAND AND A TATTOO ARTIST. I WAS THE GUINEA PIG FOR THAT ARTIST. I HELD MY OWN LIP, AND HE TATTOOED IT. PUNK ROCKERS HAVE HAD OTHER WORDS THERE, BUT I'VE NEVER SEEN ANYBODY WITH

"PUNK" tattooed on their lip.

WHEN I WAS 17, 18 YEARS OLD
I WAS SENTENCED TO 16 YEARS IN PRISON
FOR EIGHT ARMED ROBBERIES.

I WAS captured in Tasmania, and I spent seven months in prison there in solitary confinement before they transferred me to Queensland prison for security reasons. I spent the rest of my time there until I was released. To be exact, I spent seven years in maximum-security prison and one year in work release. In work release, you go out for the day and work, and then you have to come back for the night. We were robbing SportsTabs, places where people make bets in Australia. I can't say what motivated me to do it; circumstances, I guess. I was angry at society, and I just lashed out. I was on a path of self-destruction. People hurt themselves in different ways, sometimes directly through taking pills or cutting their wrists or using drugs; robbery was my way. I knew I was going to get captured. It finally happened when I was in a bank, drawing some money out. I think someone recognized me; it wasn't hard, because of my size. I'm 6'10". I was always big for my age; I was always about a foot taller than the rest of the kids. And I was always very strong naturally. When I was in prison, they started introducing weights, and we started a powerlifting club. They let me out to compete in competitions, and I started winning and breaking records in my weight division and my age division. When I was released from prison, I got invited to the World's Strongest Man competition at the Highland Games in Scotland in 1995.

I was looking for something exciting to do, and I enjoyed the athletics of the wrestling and getting in there and thrashing around. So I sent a videotape to WWE of me in the World's Strongest Man competition, and they said they were interested. I came to America and trained in UPW for about four months, and WWE offered me a development contract. But I had problems with my visa, because of my past, and it took me about 12 months to get back to the United States. During that time, I wrestled in Japan. It's a different style there. They like to use more martial arts, more high-flying maneuvers, and they like to get really physical. It was good training for me.

I MET SARA WHEN I WAS DOING AN AUTOGRAPH SESSION IN SAN DIEGO.

SHE LIVED in Orange County, and she brought two kids to an autograph session I was doing in San Diego. These kids were huge wrestling fans, and they had lost both of their parents in a car wreck. As we were pulling up in the limousine, there was a huge line wrapped around the building. I saw her in line, and I turned to Jim Dotson, our security guy who was with me, and said, "Look in this line. Who doesn't fit? Who's sticking out?" He goes, "The blonde with the black skirt" — her hair was blonde back then. When she got up through the line with the kids, I kinda struck up a conversation with her. One thing led to another, and we ended up going out and found out that we had all these things in common. We're both huge boxing fans, and we both love Ultimate Fighting Challenge and wrestling. I don't want to say Sara's unladylike, but her interests are very male oriented. It's like having a buddy and a wife. Football, anything physical like that, we sit and watch together. And she's knowledgeable about all of it; you don't have to sit there and explain things to her. In fact, we get into arguments about who knows more about boxing, me or her. And she'll tell me that she's forgotten more about boxing than I'll ever know. She's been a real turning point in my life.

Getting my "Sara" tattoo, on my throat, was just a way of showing how committed I was to her and this relationship.

A WEDDING RING, YOU CAN TAKE OFF, YOU CAN HIDE.

But my "Sara" tattoo is out there in full view where everybody can see it all the time.

I DON'T WEAR TURTLENECKS.

If something happens between us,

I'LL JUST HAVE TO FIND ANOTHER WOMAN NAMED SARA.

THE TATTOOS have been an ongoing process, a work in progress. I would sit down six, eight hours at a time and get tattoo work done. Most of it was done in Las Vegas at the Las Vegas Tattoo Company. When I started getting them, I really dug skulls. I've got skulls, demons, dragons, wizards — there's kind of a medieval flavor to the whole thing. I wasn't thinking about developing my wrestling character when I got them. It was a personal thing, but it did kind of fit into what I was doing on TV. I've seen guys get their wrestling names tattooed on them — what a big mistake that is. I was smart enough to realize that wrestling names and gimmicks change. Everything I've had done had to do with where I was in my life at the time and what I wanted. Sara asked me the other day if I ever regretted getting them. I don't, not as long as they don't get saggy and hang on me. But maybe I'll have a different answer when I'm 60.

RVP D 1.

RVP

RVP D 2.

CBCCAF-RGEC

I GOT MOST OF MY TATTOOS MY FIRST YEAR AFTER COLLEGE.

I didn't want to be all tattooed-up in college, but I knew that some day I was going to get tattoos. This is just the beginning; I just ain't had time to get any more. I got most of them in Louisville when I was down there training in Ohio Valley Wrestling. I got all of them done at the same place — Uncle Bob's Tattoo Shop — and by the same guy. He did a real good job for me. The skull thing goes back to when I was a young kid. I was always into skulls. I grew up on a farm, and we had a lot of acres and a lot of cattle. When there was a cow skeleton or skull, I'd always go and see it. I don't know what my parents think about the tattoos. I don't know what they think about me, really. But they love me, I know.

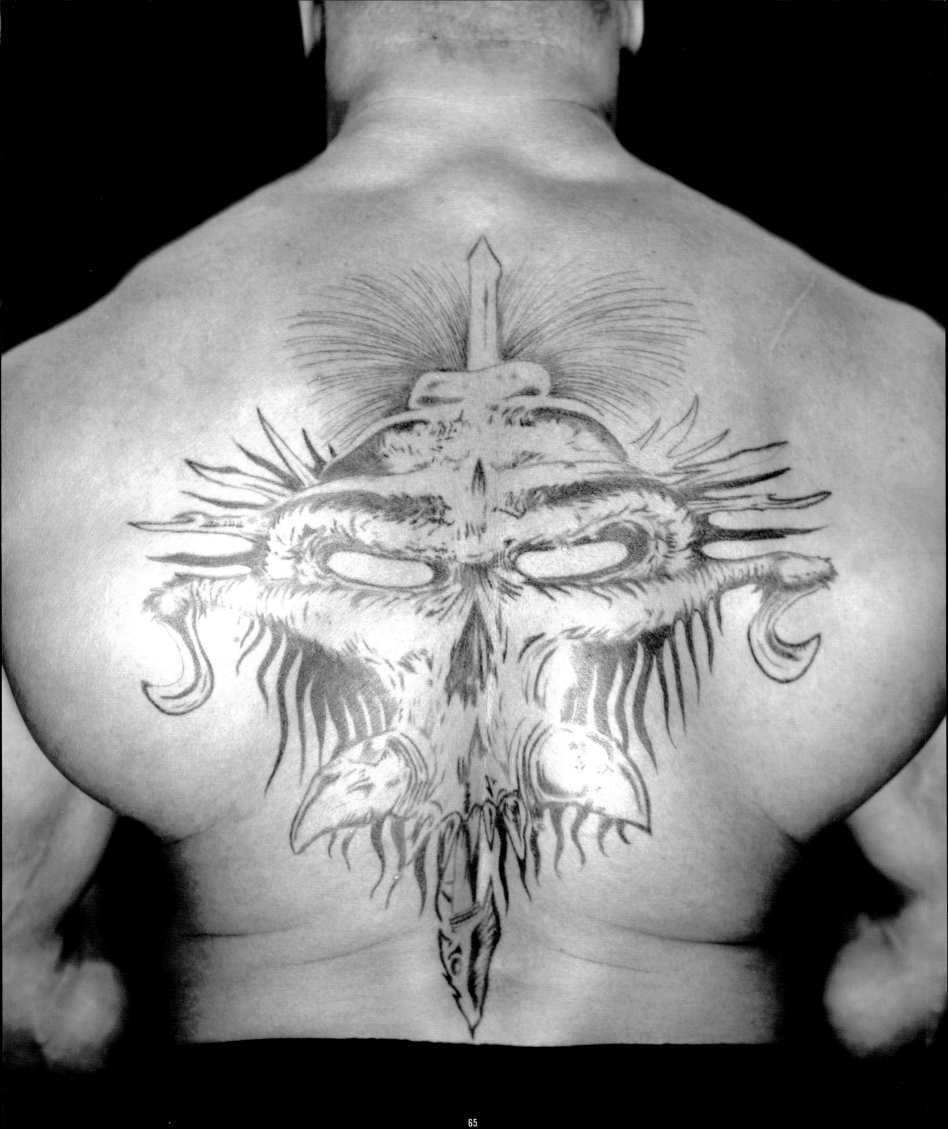

ABOUT THE time I turned 18, a guy came into the gym one day named Ted Arcidi. In 1985, he was the first guy to bench-press 700 pounds — he did 705. He got into wrestling off of that, and I met him on the downswing of his wrestling career. I was still a huge wrestling fan, but meeting him kinda made me realize,

"TED'S LIKE A REAL GUY, AND HE ACTUALLY DID THIS AS A JOB."

That's the first time it really hit me that the guys I watched on TV actually were just people. So I would pick Ted's brain about the business all the time and started bugging him, "How do you get into it?" He tried to discourage me, but eventually he pointed me in the right direction. I went to Killer Kowalski's school in Malden, Massachusetts. Killer's school, back in the day, only took very select guys. Later, when I was coming in, he was pretty much taking anybody. If you had two grand, he'd let you in. The guys all were 5'8", 5'7", 175 pounds, 180 pounds. I walked in the door at 270 pounds, and Walter — that's his real name — kinda lit up. He took a very keen interest in me. A lot of guys, he would just sit in his chair and half fall asleep while they were in the ring. When I'd get in, he'd get right up and come in the ring with me and he'd work with me very hands-on. I remember my girlfriend at the time asking me when I came out after that first day,

"WHAT ARE YOU THINKING?" I SAID, "HONEST TO GOD,
IT WAS THE MOST AT-HOME I'D EVER FELT DOING SOMETHING. IT JUST FELT NATURAL TO ME."

I never went through what a lot of guys did, like going to foreign countries and getting stuck there, sleeping in their car, down to your last dollar. I never had to go through that, because I kinda got it right away.

I WAS SUPPOSED TO BECOME A DOCTOR, BACK IN 1997.

I WAS finishing up my last year of university, where I was studying biology/kinesiology and getting ready for my MCATs to hopefully go on to med school. But the professors at my university went on strike. My only goal in life was to become a doctor, and everything I did was getting me ready for that, so for the first time in my life, I sat around with nothing to do, waiting for school to come back in session. Just to kill time until school came back, I got a job as a receptionist at a gym, and during that time, I met the publisher of *MuscleMag International* magazine and he asked me, "Do you want to do some fitness modeling?" I had been asked a couple of times when I was growing up to do the Miss Teen Canada contest, but it didn't interest me because I didn't see a viable future in it. But this time, I said, "I've got nothing to do; I'll give it a shot." Within two years, I became a 20-time cover girl; they packaged and sold me as the newest and hottest fitness model. I swear everything happens for a reason: If those professors hadn't gone on strike, I would have never pursued the modeling, which led to the wrestling industry.

I've broken my nose three times and banged it so many times that it's almost a whole different nose than when I started. Someone said, "Well, you got a pretty cheap nose job." I'm lucky, because it's turned out to be straighter than it was before. I chipped a piece of bone in my ankle — that was probably my most serious injury, only because I had to have surgery and it took me out of action for about three months. I've had many injuries that I just wrestled through. I dislocated and partially tore ligaments in my thumb; we ended up putting a brace on it and turning it into a storyline. I'm constantly bruised, but that just goes with the territory.

MY FATHER, my uncles on my mother's side, my brothers all wrestled. I am the youngest, and there wasn't a question that I wanted to do it, too. But when my big dreams were coming to me right out of high school, it was a time that if you weren't 6-foot-7, 300 pounds, you weren't even gonna be looked at. I knew I could wrestle, but my goals were always in Mexico and in Japan. To be in one of the big companies, at my size, was so far-fetched that I didn't even dream about it.

I think society doesn't understand the disease of addiction. It is a disease, and there's no prejudice to it. I was in rehab with lawyers, doctors, people that do surgery in ER. So, do I want to say that wrestling is to blame for my problems? No, it wasn't. It happens everywhere. I was drinking for a long time. Pain pills and alcohol — those were my drugs of choice. You try to get through your injuries with pain pills, but maybe if it hadn't been pain pills, I would have been drinking more, or it could have been something else. It's more of a brain disease, a behavior pattern. In my recovery group, my sponsor tells me, "You've got a harder thing to work through" — but it's possible. And I'm doing it, by the grace of God. I have to look for spiritual strength to do it, because when I've tried to do it on my own, I can't. God has blessed me with 17 months, 18 when this one is over, of being sober and drug-free. I used to count by days, and then weeks. Now, I go by months, and I look forward to when I can go by years. I'm just thankful because I have today.

I HAD MY PERSONAL DEMONS;
I STILL HAVE THEM;
BUT I'M LEARNING TO HANDLE THEM.

He's our GIANT.
He's our SHREK."

I'M SEVEN feet tall in my bare feet, and I weigh 453 pounds. My dad was 6'5'', my mom was 5'10''. The milkman was 6'10'', a hairy guy, real big through the shoulders, big head — draw your own conclusions. Seriously, my dad has the big genes. He and his first wife have a daughter, my half sister, who is 6'2''. She's got the brains in the family, very bright, a Mensa member.

I grew up in Aiken, South Carolina, which is a small town, which made me stand out even more as I grew and grew. I had a kindergarten teacher who was like 4'10'', and I think I looked her right in the eye. At 12, I was 6'2'', 220 pounds; at 14, I was 6'8'', about 235. I was real thin, but big boned, just not filled out yet. I could take two steps and dunk a basketball when I started the eighth grade, but I couldn't dribble and dunk it off the run. I didn't have enough coordination to dunk in a game, but I had enough to do it in warm-ups, which was bizarre for an eighth grader.

In junior high and when I first got to high school, I found it very hard socially to get along. In my school, anything different wasn't cool. I was a lot bigger than everybody else, and I went to school wearing work boots, Dickies work pants, and flannel shirts that were hand-me-downs from

my dad, because I was big enough to wear his stuff. All the other kids had designer jeans and Members Only jackets. What I was wearing wasn't cool. My dad was very strict, so I had a flattop, military haircut — God forbid if it touched my collar, he'd have had an aneurysm right there on the spot. I read a lot; I read through most of my junior high years. I withdrew a lot from other kids because of the teasing. I had a short temper, and if somebody messed with me, I didn't know how to handle it and just blow it off. My first rule of thumb was: "You hurt my feelings, and I'm beating the snot out of you."

I was a monster, no doubt about it. I could walk through the lunch line, walk through the playground, and kids would just part. I wasn't with the "in" crowd, so I had real nerdy friends. The really smart kids wound up hanging out with me because obviously nobody was gonna give me any trouble. I was just so damn tickled to have anybody to talk to, to hang out with. It wasn't until I started playing basketball that I got popular around school. Then, all of a sudden, this incredibly oversized kid served a purpose. It was like, "He makes the school look good, helps us win games,

I WAS GOING TO A SMALL SCHOOL IN TORONTO, HUMBER COLLEGE, AND I TOOK SOME OF MY MONEY FROM MY STUDENT LOAN AND PAID FOR WRESTLING SCHOOL.

IT WAS $2,000 OR $2,500. I'M SURE I WAS BREAKING SOME LAW,

BUT I WAS DESPERATE TO GET SOME TRAINING. MY BEST FRIEND, ADAM COPELAND, HE'S EDGE NOW, HAD GOTTEN FREE LESSONS BECAUSE HE WON AN ESSAY CONTEST ON "WHY I WANT TO BE A WRESTLER.

WE HAD ALWAYS SAID WE WERE GOING TO DO IT TOGETHER.

I moved to Adam's town in the sixth grade, and we found out we both huge wrestling fans and became instant friends. At the time, wrestling was in a huge boom;

it seemed like everybody in our school was into wrestling. But as we grew older, there were only a few of us that stayed fans. We'd wrestle around the neighborhood;

little kids would know to go and hide somewhere whenever they saw us coming, because we probably would grab them and practice our finishing moves on them.

IT WASN'T really until I got into the business that I realized how tough of a road it is to actually make a living doing it. I had to take second jobs. I worked at a wood mill, one of those jobs where you were there at 7 in the morning and didn't leave until 4 in the afternoon. I was pushing wood through saws, stacking wood and strapping it to skids, bar-coding the wood, swabbing the floors, everything. I would sit in the lunchroom and look at guys that had been working there 20, 25 years and were doing the same job as I was. It was a reality check for me; it made me realize I really had to go for what I wanted. I didn't want to end up like one of those guys. I was two or three years into wrestling before I didn't have to have another job, but it wasn't really a case of being financially able to quit everything else. It was because my parents let me stay at their house, so I didn't have to pay rent. I was wrestling every weekend and sometimes going on tours for two, three weeks at a time. So I was making enough to get by on my own, but if I had had a car payment or rent to pay, I would have had to have another job. I never really questioned myself about being able to make it in wrestling. When I got three to four years into it, it was like, "Man, I've come to far too look back." It added even more fuel to the fire because, "If I don't make it, I'm really gonna be in trouble because I haven't made a Plan B." So I didn't look at it like there was any other option. I had to make it; it was the only thing I had going for myself.

OUR BAND IS CALLED FOZZY

We got it started just as I was finishing up with WCW. My contract had four months left and I didn't re-sign, so in their infinite wisdom they punished me by giving me four months off of TV with full pay. So I wasn't working, but I was making full pay. I called up Rich Ward, who I had met at WCW; he had a band called Stuck Mojo and had done some work with Diamond Dallas Page and had played on *Nitro*. I told Rich we should put together a band and have some fun and play some of our favorite cover songs, and that's what we started to do. After we played a couple of gigs, we realized that (a) people were really into it and (b) we were a really good, kick-ass, rock 'n' roll band, so we decided to take it a little bit further. We came up with this concept that all the cover songs we were playing were really our songs that were stolen from us while we were stuck in Japan for 20 years on a bad record deal. All the other bands were stealing our songs and making millions while we were broke and destitute living in Tokyo. Then after 20 years we came back here to reclaim our crowns as the kings of heavy metal. Some record companies got onto us and got into a little bit of a bidding war, and we got signed to a record deal sight unseen. They hadn't seen us, they hadn't heard us; they just liked the fact that that Stuck Mojo, which was Rich's old band, and Chris Jericho had joined up in a band and had this whole storyline, Blues Brothers/*Spinal Tap*-type thing. We since have relaxed the storyline because the band has really gained a lot of fans and prominence. We've played a lot of good shows and sold almost 100,000 records worldwide between our two albums.

WHEN MY HAIR STARTED LEAVING ME, I ACTUALLY WENT TO HAIR CLUB FOR MEN
AND I LET THE LADY THERE COMB THROUGH MY HAIR WITH A COUPLE OF THOSE WOODEN TONGUE DEPRESSORS.

I DECIDED THAT WASN'T THE THING FOR ME, SO I CUT MY HAIR REAL SHORT.

IT WAS KIND OF A PRETTY-BOY LOOK, BUT THAT WASN'T VERY GOOD FOR ME.

WHEN I WAS CONTACTED BY WWE TO COME UP AND BE THE RINGMASTER, THEY WANTED ME TO CHANGE MY LOOK.
"PULP FICTION" WAS OUT AT THAT TIME, SO BASICALLY I KIND OF COPIED BRUCE WILLIS' BUZZ HAIRCUT;

I DIDN'T HAVE THE GOATEE YET.

ONE TIME IN PHILADELPHIA, I DECIDED TO SHAVE ALL MY HAIR OFF.

WHEN I DID IT, I DIDN'T HAVE THIS CRAZY-SHAPED HEAD; I ACTUALLY HAD A PRETTY COOL-SHAPED HEAD.
THEN I FINALLY DECIDED TO GROW THE GOATEE IN, AND THE WHOLE LOOK JUST KINDA FELL TOGETHER.

AS FAR as letting fans know what's going on behind the scenes with me, I have no problem with that. Any aspect of my life that they want to know about, I'll have an answer. If I have a fork or a cell phone in my hand, I like to be left alone then, but otherwise I'm pretty much open access, 24-7. That kinda comes and goes with the territory in WWE. I've always liked to know about the rock stars. I'm a big music fan, country music and roll 'n' roll, and I always want to know what they do behind the scenes.

SECTION II

BODY

It's not hard on me physically, never has been really. Guys say they're sore the next day after a match; I'm not, unless I've haven't done it for a while. The old saying is:

"TIME OFF IS A WRESTLER'S

WORST ENEMY."

WHEN I'M bumping around on a regular basis, I feel fine. Probably the worst thing that's happened to me was I broke my back in an airplane crash in 1975. Then I cracked C5 in my neck in 1987. I thought that was gonna be serious, but it healed itself, although it was painful. I didn't miss a day of work with that; they put me in tag matches every night and I just stood in the corner for about a month. I had my gall-bladder removed in 1976, which wasn't because of the business, although indirectly it was because it probably was because of the plane crash. I've had both of my rotator cuffs repaired, which were major repairs. But that's all minor stuff for this business. I've got no knee, back, elbow problems, like a lot of guys do. I'm pain-free; no discomfort. I feel absolutely phenomenal.

MY TRAINING REGIMEN IS PRETTY SIMPLE. BASICALLY, I DO 45 MINUTES OF CARDIO, WITH A PUNCHING ROUTINE, SOME QUICK, RUNNING SPURTS, AND SOME LUNGES IN THERE, TOO. THAT COVERS MY CARDIOVASCULAR TRAINING, AND I'M ALSO ISOMETRICALLY TRAINING MY MUSCLES.

I'VE BUILT UP A PRETTY GOOD FOUNDATION FROM MY FITNESS-MODEL DAYS SO THAT NOW I CAN JUST BASICALLY MAINTAIN EVERYTHING. THERE'S NO EXCUSE TO MISS A WORKOUT WHEN ALL I'VE GOT TO DO IS FIND A TREADMILL; THERE'S ALWAYS A HOTEL GYM WHERE I CAN GET IN MY 45 MINUTES.

Trish Stratus
PATRICIA ANNESTRATIGIAS

I **FEEL** so hurt right now, my bones. I wake up in the morning, I ache. I can't believe that I'm only 28 — but I've been wrestling for 13 years. When I'm hurting, it makes me feel like I'm old, and I don't like that feeling. I've had four surgeries on my left knee — it's bad. I talked to the trainer. I said, "Larry, my knee goes click, click — it snaps all the time. I'll be sitting down and as I get up, 'Oh, oh, it's caught!' And I'll hear a snap." And the trainer told me, "Well, your cartilage is pretty much all gone. Eventually you're gonna need a knee replacement." I don't want that. And he goes, "Well, you're gonna need it." But I feel healthy if I can move and I can go in the ring and I can perform, so as long as I have that and the blessing of God, I'm good to go. I might be hurting; I might be aching, sore — but, hell, we all can get up from that.

NO MATTER HOW MUCH THEY TELL ME, "REY, SLOW DOWN, YOU'RE GONNA GET HURT. REY, YOU'RE HURT, TAKE CARE OF YOURSELF" — I JUST DON'T LISTEN. I LIKE TO GO OUT THERE AND I LIKE TO GIVE MORE THAN 100 PERCENT, AND THAT'S THE WAY IT'S GONNA BE, ALWAYS.

IT TAKES a toll on the body, man, when you do 250, 270 days a year. All the traveling, then bumping night after night in that ring. My knees are bad; my lower back is really shot. But that's what 14 years in the business will do to you.

My lower back is in bad shape — I'll need to get something done with it at some point. I've heard about a new technique where they inject something into your disk that blows it up. When it gets down there to the spinal cord, I get really scared and freaked out. I do therapy on my back and try to take care of it, and not land on it. It wasn't one thing that did it; it's all the years I've been landing on it. Go out in the yard and jump off of something and land on your back — do that every day. Now you know what we do to ourselves.

I once hyperextended my knee so bad I had to have surgery on it. It was in England or Germany, I can't remember. I came down on it, and the thing bent back like an accordion and I just crumbled. It scared me to death. Scary times, scary moments in the business.

MY LEFT HAND GOT MESSED UP PRETTY BAD. I WAS WRESTLING ROAD DOGG IN 1997 OR '98. I GAVE HIM A BULLDOG, WHICH IS ONE OF MY MOVES THAN I'VE DONE A BILLION TIMES. I HAPPENED TO LAND ON MY HAND BACKWARDS, AND I CUT ALL THE METACARPALS. THEY WERE CORKSCREW BREAKS; THEY ALL SNAPPED, EVERY ONE OF THEM. I WENT THROUGH A FIVE-HOUR SURGERY WHERE THEY PUT TWO PINS IN EACH FINGER AND WRAPPED THEM IN WIRE. WHAT YOU SEE NOW IS SCAR TISSUE. IT WAS JUST ONE OF THOSE INCIDENTS WHERE YOU LAND WRONG. PEOPLE THINK IT'S SO EASY, BUT THERE'S ALWAYS THAT CHANCE OF MESSING UP. YOU CAN ACCIDENTALLY HIT A GUY AND KNOCK HIM OUT, OR BREAK HIS NECK. THERE'VE BEEN A LOT OF BROKEN NECKS AROUND HERE LATELY.

I broke my neck in 1996. I had two herniated disks, a bruised spinal cord and five pulled muscles in my neck.

THIS WAS THREE MONTHS BEFORE THE OLYMPICS.

I made it through that, won the gold medal at the Olympics, took a three-year period off, then joined WWE.

FROM THEN on, every week my neck was getting worse and worse, but I didn't tell anybody. One morning I woke up and couldn't raise my arm; it felt like I had a really bad pinched nerve. But what happened is that my nerve just shut down. That was about five weeks before *WrestleMania*, which is not the right time for it to happen. I got approval from my doctor to wrestle one more match, because I had the title and you just can't go, "Hey, who wants the title?" You have to somehow have someone beat you for it. So I said, "If I'm wrestling one more match, I'm wrestling at *WrestleMania*; I'm not gonna give up the title at a house show or on *SmackDown!*" So I did very limited action on TV for five weeks, then at *WrestleMania* I went out there and did whatever I could. It wasn't my best performance, but I was happy. I hate to say it, but guys in this business, they have egos. At points, you feel indestructible, like nothing can hurt you — and that's what happened with me. I let my ego get in the way, and I'm a team player. To me, being in this business isn't about wi ning or losing; it's about putting on the best product possible, and I felt that the best match of the night was going to be Brock Lesnar-Kurt Angle, regardless of my neck being hurt. I wanted to do it not just for me, but for the company. Vince McMahon discouraged me, but it was ultimately my choice, and when I decided to do it, he thanked me.

IN THIS BUSINESS, YOU'RE GOING TO GET INJURED
THIS ISN'T BALLET.

ALL YOU CAN PRAY FOR IS THAT IT'S NOT TOO SERIOUS. I BROKE MY LEG — BIG DEAL; YOU WALK AROUND OUR LOCKER ROOM, THAT'S NOTHING, ABSOLUTELY NOTHING COMPARED TO SOME OF THE INJURIES THESE GUYS HAVE EXPERIENCED. THE NECK SURGERIES ALONE ARE COUNTLESS. BUT WHEN YOU COME BACK AND THE FANS HAVEN'T SEEN YOU IN A WHILE, THE REACTION YOU GET WHEN YOU GO OUT THERE AGAIN MAKES ALL THOSE HOURS OF REHAB WORTH IT.

93

DOING THE HIGH-RISK STUFF, THE REALLY EXCITING, DANGEROUS MOVES, BEING THE DARE-DEVILS, THERE'S NO DOUBT THAT'S WHAT PUT JEFF AND I ON THE MAP AS THE HARDY BOYZ.

Being smaller guys, we know we've got to be a little special and work harder. On the other hand, doing what we do definitely makes us more susceptible to being injured. We do complicated stuff, stuff that people 20 years ago never dreamed about doing. And Jeff and I were the pioneers of that in a lot of ways. Problem is, the more you do, the more the people want. The days of the 350-pound guy who just stands in the ring and looks menacing are gone. People these days are so educated and so smart about wrestling, when they pay, they want to be entertained, not only by a character and a funny or dramatic scenario, they also want to see a high-quality athletic contest.

WHEN YOU'RE OUT THERE, YOU DON'T THINK ABOUT WHAT'S HAPPENING TO YOUR BODY. BUT WHEN YOU'RE AWAY FROM IT, SOMETIMES YOU THINK ABOUT 20, 30 YEARS FROM NOW. WE'RE GONNA BE BAD ENOUGH OFF PHYSICALLY, AS IT IS. WHATEVER WE CAN DO TO CUT BACK ON THE HIGH-RISK STUFF, WE SHOULD BE THINKING ABOUT DOING. YOU'VE JUST GOT TO BE SMART ABOUT IT. BECAUSE AS COOL AND AS GREAT AS IT IS TO WRESTLE, THERE'S A LONG LIFE AFTER WRESTLING, AND YOU DON'T WANT TO BE CRIPPLED AND COMPLETELY MISERABLE FROM IT.

YOU CAN ARGUE THAT FOOTBALL AND WRESTLING ARE EQUALLY DANGEROUS

IN FOOTBALL, EVERY PLAY CAN BE YOUR LAST.

EVEN THOUGH WRESTLING IS CHOREOGRAPHED, YOU CAN'T CONTROL EVERYTHING
THAT HAPPENS WHEN BIG, WELL-CONDITIONED, ATHLETIC GUYS ARE CRASHING INTO EACH OTHER.

EVERYBODY GETS HURT OUT THERE
— IT'S JUST TO WHAT EXTENT THEY GET HURT.

THE CONSTANT POUNDING ON YOUR BODY WEEK AFTER WEEK AFTER WEEK AFTER
WEEK AFTER WEEK AFTER WEEK MAKES YOUR BODY MORE PRONE TO INJURY.

IN FOOTBALL, IF YOU GO DOWN, THERE'S A GUY RIGHT BEHIND YOU WHO CAN STEP IN AND FILL YOUR SHOES.

HERE, YOU SUCK IT UP AND KEEP GOING, PLAY THOUGH YOUR INJURIES.

Goldberg
BILL GOLDBERG

I TOOK A KENDO STICK SHOT
in the back of the neck in ECW from Bubba Ray Dudley. It was just one of those heat-of-the-moment things.

HE WAS swinging for my head, and I didn't realize it and bent over, and he ended up catching me right in the back of the neck. I went a little tingly for a minute — that was pretty frightening. I got neck-collared, back-boarded, and dragged off to the hospital for X-rays. Fortunately, it turned out to be just a spinal bruise, which doesn't sound fortunate, but in the long term was harmless.

I joke about it, but I'm actually quite serious: One of my goals is to retire surgery-free, which would actually be a helluva accomplishment. The physical standards have been raised so high in this industry. I've worked in ECW, which had such a rep for violence, and I worked in Japan for a lot of years, which is a very physically demanding area. So if I can make it my last how many years without surgery, I think it very well could be some kind of a record.

MY BICEPS ARE THE LARGEST IN THE WORLD.

I DON'T EVER MEASURE THEM — I DON'T EVER CHECK MY WEIGHT, EITHER — BECAUSE IT'S TOO PSYCHOLOGICAL.

Scott Steiner
SCOTT RECHSTEINER

If you measure them every day, you get paranoid. I actually could be a lot bigger right now if I wanted to, but it would hamper my wrestling - the mobility and stuff like that. I'm not as big as I could be, but I'm big enough. I've been working out since after my freshman year of wrestling in high school. And believe it or not, I've never missed a workout. I might have missed a day, maybe had to do it later, but I've never missed a workout. When I first started, I just tried to get as big as I could; I never worried about being cut. But when I worked on getting cut, that's when I really got bigger. There's so many factors involved to look this way. I could work out and not watch my diet, and I wouldn't look the same. If you slack off on one, you can't expect to get the best results. It takes a lot of dedication to be ripped.

I work out six days a week, one body part a day, along with cardio every day. Monday, I do triceps. Tuesday, I do chest, stuff on the bench. Wednesday is biceps, then back, then shoulders, and then legs, I do about 5 different exercises each day because I want to hit it at different angles, in 3 sets, usually 10 reps. The lifting takes an hour to an hour and a half. Then I do about 30 minutes of cardio.

IT'S HARDER TO DO WHEN YOU'RE TRAVELING, AND MAYBE SOME GUYS SLACK OFF A LITTLE,
BUT THAT JUST SEPARATES THE MEN FROM THE BOYS.

I'M SURE I'M GOING TO HAVE SOME PHYSICAL PROBLEMS DOWN THE LINE

— BUT SOMETIMES YOU SEE REGULAR PEOPLE, TOO, ALL BROKEN DOWN WHEN THEY'RE 50 OR 60. I DO THE BEST THAT I CAN TO TAKE CARE OF MY BODY, BUT IT'S BROKEN DOWN. I'VE HAD NECK SURGERY, ELBOW SURGERY. BUT FOR THE MOST PART, I FEEL PRETTY GOOD, CONSIDERING THAT I'VE BEEN DOING THIS FOR 18 YEARS.

Chris Benoit

I THINK A LOT OF IT IS STATE OF MIND. I REALLY BELIEVE THAT IN THIS INDUSTRY YOUR BODY DEVELOPS A HIGH PAIN TOLERANCE. TAKE MY NECK, FOR INSTANCE. RIGHT AFTER THE SURGERY — THEY FUSED C6 AND C7 — IT FELT SO GOOD, I THOUGHT, "OH MY GOD! I CAN'T BELIEVE I WAS ABLE TO FUNCTION WITH THAT MUCH PAIN." FOR A LONG TIME BEFORE I HAD THE SURGERY, I WENT THROUGH A PERIOD OF DENIAL. NOT TO SAY I'M BIGGER OR BADDER THAN ANYONE ELSE — ALL THE GUYS HAVE NAGGING INJURIES AND CHRONIC PAIN; YOU JUST LEARN TO LIVE WITH IT AND YOU WORK THROUGH IT. NOT TO SAY THAT THE PEOPLE DON'T APPRECIATE WHAT WE GO THROUGH, BUT I REALLY DON'T BELIEVE THAT ANYONE OUTSIDE THE BUSINESS CAN GRASP JUST HOW DEMANDING IT IS PHYSICALLY WHAT WE DO TO OURSELVES ON A NIGHTLY BASIS. AND WE HAVE NO OFF-SEASON TO RECOVER.

IT USED TO BE YOU HAD BIG, RAWBONED GUYS, AND SOME GUYS HAD BEER GUTS.

NOW, EVERYBODY PUTS IN THEIR TIME IN THE GYM.
THEY REALIZE THAT AN ELEMENT OF THE BUSINESS THAT'S GOTTEN REAL BIG IS,

"LOOKS DO MATTER." YOUR PHYSICAL APPEARANCE DOES MATTER;

IT MATTERS WITH VINCE MCMAHON. VINCE IS A BODYBUILDER; HE PUTS IN HIS TIME IN THE GYM.
IF YOU CAN IMPRESS HIM, YOU'RE OPENING THE DOOR A LITTLE WIDER FOR YOURSELF.
AND WHEN SOMEBODY ON OUR ROSTER ISN'T IN SHAPE, THEY HEAR ABOUT IT.

MY WHOLE eye socket is titanium mesh; it's all rebuilt in there. I was wrestling Mabel, who was 6'8" and 450, 500 pounds, maybe more. I took a clothesline from him that pretty much ended up as a fist in the eye, and it crushed my eye socket. He was moving toward me and I was going toward him, and his fist just got me first. When I breathed, my face would fill up with air. My mindset at the time, the way I did things, was that if you could walk, you could work, you could go to the ring, and that's what I did. I worked three more days. When I got into the optometrist and they looked at it, they told me if I had taken another shot in that eye that I would have lost it, because the nerves and everything were rubbing up against a jagged piece of bone.

I TRY to eat high protein and low carb, but I refuse to be an egg-whites-and-chicken-breast guy and nothing but. The one pleasure I still keep is my eating habits. I'll eat fish and chicken, but I love red meat and I eat it when I want it. I try to really cut my carb consumption after 3 or 4 in the afternoon. I don't eat cereal at night anymore — that was my favorite nighttime junk food. I do a lot of cardio to try and keep the fat down. But I'm not as strict as a lot of guys. I'll eat a piece of fried chicken in a heartbeat. I make enough sacrifices in my daily routine that if I want to eat something, I'm going to. That's not saying I'm gonna eat 30 pieces of fried chicken, but I am gonna take care of that craving, and if that means doing extra cardio the next day, so be it. When Sara and I first moved in together, she'd cook three square meals a day, plus dessert at night. When I hurt my pecs — I was originally out because of a groin tear, and when I was rehabbing that, I tore my pecs — I was 350 pounds, heaviest I'd ever been. I was training like an animal, with heavy weights, but Sara was feeding me so well, I was enormous.

DO NOT ENT   SIDE

tore my ACL during the Chicago Street Fight that Trish Stratus and I had. I slammed her on a trashcan lid. She rolled out of the way, and I landed on the trashcan lid, and my knee went into the trashcan part that doesn't bend. I didn't take any time off — I just wear a brace on my knee now when I wrestle. I talked to Stone Cold and he inspired me. He said, "As long as you wear your brace and train your muscles to work out your ACL, you're fine; just be aware of what you're doing."

NOT TO COMPARE MYSELF TO STONE COLD OR ANYTHING, BUT IF HE CAN DO IT, I CAN DO IT.

ight before going down the ramp, I'm always praying to God that I don't hurt myself or that the other person does not get really injured. But my main thought is that I want to kick some butt and entertain the fans. Really, injury is the last thing on my mind.

SHE DIDN'T SEE THE PAY-PER-VIEW, AND SHE SAID, "WHAT'S GOING ON?"
AND I SAID, "I ALMOST GOT PARALYZED TONIGHT."
OF COURSE, SHE DIDN'T EVEN GET THE GRAVITY OF THE SITUATION.

I GOT dropped on my head in 1997 wrestling against Owen Hart at *SummerSlam*. I was almost paralyzed; I was a transient quadriplegic for 90 seconds. I bruised my spinal cord; I was lucky I didn't sever it. It was a piledriver gone bad, an accident. It was a severe actual load, which is your number one cause for quadriplegics. I was in real good shape at the time, and I consider myself pretty tough, but the bottom line, 99 percent of why I'm not paralyzed is I was lucky. As I watched the tape, I saw that I could pick my head up off the mat, but nothing else worked. My hands were drawn up; my legs were straight. Immediately, the first thing I thought about was Christopher Reeve, because he had already had his accident. I couldn't move — I thought that was it. We were supposed to work 5 or 6 or 7 minutes longer, and I was gonna win the match with a Stunner for the Intercontinental Championship. By all rights, I should have just laid there and waited for the MDs to come and give me the proper assistance. But I was thinking of the business; I was thinking of the show. We were on Pay-Per-View; Continental Airlines Arena in Meadowlands, New Jersey, was sold out — I was looking to finish the match. Finally, I started getting a little bit of movement back. I couldn't crawl on my hands; I could barely crawl on my elbows — if you watch the tape, it's a real piece of work. I told the referee, "Hey, a roll-up for the win," and I rolled up Owen. It was everything that I could do to even bend my legs, because they were stuck straight. They helped me up, and I held the belt up. I dragged my legs backstage, and I got pretty emotional back there. Then they took me to the hos-

pital and gave me some X-rays. Two or three wrestling fans actually took me back to my hotel because I didn't have a ride; the ambulance didn't take me back. My anterior delts, the front of my shoulders, were burning, on fire, like someone put Icy Hot on them. I was lying in bed after they brought me back to the hotel room — drinkin' a 12-pack of beer — and, man, I was shook up. And the effects started setting in from just being whammed; all the trauma started setting in. I was light-headed, weirded-out, and confused. And no one was calling. I finally called my wife at the time — I've been through a few marriages. She didn't see the Pay-Per-View, and she said, "What's going on?" And I said, "I almost got paralyzed tonight" Of course, she didn't even get the gravity of the situation.

They needed me to show up at *Raw* the next night to cut a promo, because I was Stone Cold Steve Austin and I was on my way to being very, very hot. So I cut the promo the next day, just to be on TV. My shoulders were on fire for about two weeks, and finally that subsided to an itch, and finally it left all together three or four months later. I'd go out and ride on my four-wheeler — I used to live out in the country. I rode my four-wheeler around all day and drank a case of beer — that was my rehab. The whole ordeal was very alienating for me. You start to think, "This shit ain't worth it." For a while I considered not going back. But I'd been working for 8 years, busting my ass, paying my dues, and now all of a sudden I'd come up with the Stone Cold thing, and it was fixin' to be the best thing since sliced bread. I didn't want to stop then.

I WISH THAT ACCIDENT WOULD HAVE NEVER HAPPENED, BECAUSE I'M IN A BAD WAY NOW;

I STILL SUFFER FROM THE EFFECTS. BUT IT DID HELP MY CAREER, BECAUSE PEOPLE LIKE TO SEE PEOPLE COME BACK FROM ADVERSITY, FROM INJURIES, SHOW SOME GUTS, SOME GUMPTION, WANT-TO, WHERE-WITHAL, WHATEVER. IT ACTUALLY PROBABLY HELPED MY POPULARITY, FOR SOME CRAZY REASON.

I DON'T TRAIN EVERY DAY, BUT I TRAIN REALLY, REALLY HARD. I'M NOT GETTING ANY YOUNGER,

plus I want to be the best every night; I want to go out and try to steal the show every night with my in-ring performance. To be able to do that, you've got to train a certain way, and mentally you've got to keep yourself at your peak. How I work out is pretty much according to where I am. If I'm in a hotel, I'll do pretty much an all-around body parts workout, which means I'll use what equipment they've got just to get something out of it. When I'm at home, I'll train body parts. I'll go with my back and my biceps one day, then shoulders and triceps another day. I try to do a pushing exercise and a pulling exercise. If you try to do all pushing, you're gonna be tired. If you do half pushing and half pulling, your body stays at it. My motivation is to look good and stay healthy. I don't want to grow old before my time.

I'M NOT beat-up like a lot of the wrestlers are. I've taken care of myself over the years; my joints and my bones are pretty healthy. But there are days after I've been on the road and I come home that my body's pretty stiff and I'm pretty sore, and it's tough to get out of bed. But that comes along with the territory; that's part of the job. I'm just thankful I'm not crippled or anything like that.

I had a neck injury I was pretty concerned about when I was with WCW. I got dropped on my head pretty hard in an awkward position. I was coming down on the back of my head and going forward at the same time. I was able to catch myself a little because I could see what was happening, and that probably helped me from being seriously hurt. I was in some pain, but it turned out that I was OK.

Other than that, I can't complain. I feel like I've been blessed; I feel like I've got a higher power on my side. That explains why I'm in shape, why I haven't been seriously hurt, why I've lasted 10 years on television. Most guys' careers don't go as well as mine has gone. My bumps and bruises seem to heal much quicker than they do for other people.

I started working out when I was about 20. Back at that time, I was dancing, a street dancer, and I was pretty good. But you've got younger kids coming up, and you've got to compete just that much harder. When I was 20 years old, you had 15-, 16-year-old kids doing dancing stuff that was amazing. I was going on reputation alone, as far as how good a dancer I used to be. So I felt like it was time to move into something else, because the kids were getting too good. At the time, my brother was working out all the time, and I realized he was the one who had all the pretty girls. So I decided I best try buffing up, too.

THE SCARIEST injury for me was my back. It was after the Casket match with Undertaker at the *Royal Rumble* in 1998. I was fine after the match, did the TV show the next day, went home the next morning, went to sleep that night. But when I woke up Wednesday morning, I couldn't move in bed. I couldn't even turn to get to the phone. It was like the world's hottest knife in my back. I couldn't move my legs; I couldn't turn my upper body. Every time I tried to move, it was just searing pain down my legs. All I could think was, "Make the pain go away." I was living alone in this big house, so I was stuck in bed, one of those huge four-poster beds. I had to roll myself off the bed to the floor, which hurt like you can't believe. Then I reached up and managed to grab my phone, and I called my parents and said, "I'm on the floor in my bedroom and I can't move. Call me an ambulance." It took the ambulance 20 minutes to get to the house, and my parents probably 30 minutes. From where I was on the floor, it was no more than 12 feet to my front door, and it took me 20 minutes to crawl that far, on my stomach, inch by inch. I was stuck in a flat position. I couldn't bend to get my hands up underneath me; I couldn't grab the wall to get up. I was crying; I was calling out to a God I didn't know, "Make the pain go away!" I'd never, ever felt that kind of pain in my life; every time I moved, it just shot through my body. They had to shoot me up with Demerol to get me on the gurney for the ride to the hospital. That eased everything up, but I knew something wasn't right. I found out I was going to need surgery to fuse vertebrae in my lower back. Before I could get that done, I still had to wrestle at *WrestleMania*, get through my match with Steve Austin. That was in January; *WrestleMania* was in March. They let me off of the February Pay-Per-View so I could just make it to *WrestleMania* and do the job I needed to do. About halfway through that match, I was in awful pain again. There are just some things you have to do for the business. I knew Steve was where we were going in the future, and I knew I had to go in there and make that happen. So from that standpoint, it was very noble. But I certainly can understand why somebody on the outside would say we're just incredibly dumb for taking chances like that. In my condition, if it were any other show except *WrestleMania*, you might not do it. But this was for the world title, the main event at *WrestleMania*, all those things that very few guys get a chance to do. Here you are, you've had a chance to do it a couple of times, and now you're on the other end, the part where you've got to hand that baton off; you've got to do the noble thing. And you say, "I've got to do that. I would want somebody to do that for me."

I'M AN EGG-WHITES-AND-CHICKEN-BREASTS GUY, AND A LOW-CARB GUY.

I COULD PROBABLY BE A LITTLE BIGGER, BUT AT THIS AGE, IF I CARRY A LITTLE LESS WEIGHT THAT I USED TO, IT'S BETTER FOR MY KNEES AND MY BACK,

AND KEEPING A LOW-CARB DIET HELPS ME DO THAT. THE WAY YOU LOOK IS SO IMPORTANT NOW, MORE SO THAN WHEN I GOT INTO WRESTLING; THERE WERE

A LOT OF BIG, FAT GUYS IN IT THEN. NOW, IT'S A VERY AESTHETIC BUSINESS. IT DEMANDS MORE, TOO; THE ATHLETES ARE JUST GETTING BETTER.

THERE'S A lot more at stake now than when I got into it. There's more money at stake, period. It used to be it was a line of work where you could make a living. Now it's a line of work where you can secure your future. Plain and simple, you can get rich, at least some guys can. I did what I think anybody would say was pretty darn good financially in wrestling. But now, in my second time around, it's staggering. That's why I say my God is a God of redemption, a God of second chances.

I am what I would consider to be an old-timer, and the one big difference between us and the newer guys is that the newer guys — and I don't mean this critically — don't have a genuine, genuine, genuine appreciation for the business, because I don't know that they would do it for nothing. You get your Undertaker, you get your Steve Austin — none of us got into it for the money. We got into it because we wanted to do it, and then it exploded and got so big, and we realized you could make a future, so it was even better. There was a time when I drove down the road in a beat-up car that my parents helped me get; there was a time when I was eating out of tin cans; there was a time I was staying in hotels that were not pretty. You don't have that anymore. It's not the newer guys' fault, the business has just gotten better. But to say that they have the same appreciation for it that we do, I just think that would be inaccurate. Because of the circumstances, they can't have the same appreciation.

I do cardio 6 days a week, and I train with weights 5 days. I try to do a body part a day.
I'll do 30 to 45 minutes of cardio every morning, then I'll do a body part after that. What's difficult is that I can't lift heavy anymore.

THE INJURIES AND EVERYTHING ELSE HAVE TAKEN A TOLL, AND I JUST CAN'T LIFT ANYTHING THAT HEAVY.

I've got to discipline myself to go to my gym, because I've got a 3-year-old that I'd rather play with. He understands now that Daddy's got to go to the gym first thing in the morning, and he's got me the rest of the day, so I try to get it out of the way early in the morning. Once I get into a groove, I'm pretty disciplined with my diet and training.

IT'S ONLY WHEN I GET AWAY FROM IT THAT I CAN BE REALLY LAZY.

FAKE IS NOT A WORD I LIKE TO USE
BECAUSE THERE'S NOTHING FAKE ABOUT WHAT I DO.

It's a show, it's a predetermined outcome; we're putting on a television drama, action, comedy, whatever you want to call it — but it's not fake. Fake would be if I was just about to take a body slam, and my stuntman did it. Fake would be if I was going to take a chair shot to the head, and the chair was made of rubber. I'll tell the world that it's a show, but I hate the word fake. It's such an unfair term to us.

I'M ALMOST never injured enough to be out, but I'm injured more than the average person walking down the street. I've had a bulging disk in my upper neck, a bulging disk in my lower neck. I've had a couple of sprained ankles. I have a bulging disk in my lower back, which makes my leg go numb, which is not a great feeling. Most of the time, the day after a match is when you really feel it. It's not always excruciating pain, but enough where it's hard to get out of bed in the morning. The other day when I came out of the ring, for some reason I had a huge lockup in the back of my neck, like a muscle just totally stiff. I couldn't move my neck, so it was hurting all down in my back and chest. Little things like that, it might just be a stiff muscle, but that's enough to impede your ability to be comfortable for a week or two.

The biggest injury I had was when I broke my arm in a match and had a steel plate put in with 7 screws in August of 1994. I was out for about 8 weeks. Back then, I didn't have a contract with anybody, so no one was paying my hospital bills, no one was paying anything. They told me I was going to be out for 16 weeks; I said that's unacceptable. I came back after 7 weeks.

The injury factor — of course, it's scary. Every time you step in the ring you could get seriously injured. It's like a football game or a hockey game — you never know, there's always that X-factor that something might happen. Thank God, I'm very fortunate it hasn't happened to me, and I pray it never does. I don't plan to be wrestling when I'm 40 years old; I don't want to be wrestling when I'm 40 years old.

HOPEFULLY, MY BODY WILL FORGIVE ME SO I DON'T HAVE TO WALK WITH A CANE WHEN I'M 40 YEARS OLD.

I STARTED BODYBUILDING WHEN I WAS 14, AND THAT PRETTY MUCH TOOK OVER FOR ME. THEY WANTED ME TO PLAY FOOTBALL IN HIGH SCHOOL, BUT I HAD NO INTEREST IN IT. I TRAINED AT A GYM CALLED MUSCLES IN MOTION IN NASHUA, NEW HAMPSHIRE AND ALL MY FRIENDS WERE OLDER GUYS. I REMEMBER WALKING IN THERE FOR THE FIRST TIME, AND THERE WERE A COUPLE OF GUYS THERE THAT WERE THE BIGGEST GUYS I'D EVER SEEN.

THEY PROBABLY WEREN'T EVEN THAT BIG, BUT TO ME IT WAS,
"OH MY GOD! THIS IS THE COOLEST THING I'VE EVER SEEN. I'VE GOT TO DO THIS."
I THINK I'VE ALWAYS HAD A FASCINATION WITH STRENGTH AND POWER.

ONE OF my attractions to professional wrestling was that the guys were bigger-than-life giants, superheroes. I was the youngest guy in the gym, a tall, skinny kid that just wanted to train. I'd be in there training with guys that were 250 pounds and just strong as could be. Every rep and every set — not weight-wise, obviously — that they did, I would do. If my arms were gonna fall off, I would still do it. There's just some-thing about weight training for me. It's so immediate. You do the exercise, you feel the burn, you feel the pain, and you know you're doing something. I've never been out of the gym for any period of time to speak of. I've never said, "I'm gonna take a week off because I feel like my body needs a rest." I don't miss a workout except occasionally when I'm on the road.

RVP   CBCCAF-AGEC

RVP   CBCCAF-AGEC

RVP ▷ 1.   RVP ▷ 2.

Triple H
PAUL LEVESQUE

117

I'M NOT ALL BUSTED UP LIKE A LOT OF THE GUYS ARE BECAUSE I'VE NEVER REALLY PUT MYSELF IN A LOT OF DANGER AND TAKEN A LOT OF RISK IN THE RING. I'VE NEVER VENTURED TO THE TOP ROPE, THAT'S FOR SURE. I WOULD ALWAYS RATHER CONCENTRATE ON CHARISMA AND ENERGY WHEN I PERFORM. IF I CAN EMIT ENERGY THAT NOBODY ELSE HAS — TRUTHFUL, POWERFUL ENERGY — AND MIX THAT WITH A LITTLE BIT OF CHARISMA AND WITH THE RIGHT ANTAGONIST OR PROTAGONIST,

I CAN USUALLY GET THE RIGHT CONNECTION WITH THE CROWD, AND I DON'T HAVE TO BE JUMPING OFF LADDERS.

I'M STILL AT THAT AGE WHERE I'M OBLIVIOUS TO PAIN AND OBLIVIOUS TO DYING, I THINK.

You'd think that I'd really start paying attention more to that stuff because of my daughter — I have a one-year-old daughter — but I haven't found that shut-off or that kill switch yet. I do certain things out of ignorance and for the rush.

I'VE HAD A LOT OF BAD INJURIES,
BUT LUCKILY I'VE BEEN ABLE TO BOUNCE BACK FROM THEM —

7 CONCUSSIONS, 3 BROKEN NOSES, 2 BROKEN RIBS, A SHATTERED ANKLE, STITCHES IN MY HEAD OVER 35 TIMES.

ANYTHING ELSE that needed a stitch that I didn't have time to get stitched, we took Crazy Glue and glued it back together — Sabu used to do the same thing. I shattered my ankle at the first ECW Pay-Per-View — it was called *Barely Legal* — in 1997. Opening match, the Dudleys versus the Eliminators — within the first five minutes I shattered my ankle. Stupid, simple injury. I was standing on the apron, and I jumped off to the floor, and my ankle just collapsed. I didn't know if I could get up; I didn't know if I could walk. But a shot of adrenaline came over me, and it kept me going. I'm very proud to say that I continued the rest of the match and took the Eliminators' finish — Total Elimination, which is a reverse leg sweep and a roundhouse kick to the face — with a shattered ankle. I don't mean a broken ankle; my ankle actually shattered. I've continued matches with concussions. One of the worst things that

ever happened to me in WWE was in the Tables, Ladders, and Chairs match in Las Vegas, when Chris Jericho gave me a Bulldog off a 10-foot ladder. I was completely knocked out, do not remember anything from the match, couldn't tell you where I was, how I got there — but I completed the match and managed to hit all of my spots. Jericho actually had to guide me through the rest of that match, tell me what was going on. At one point, he told me, "Go up the ladder and give Christian a Bubba Bomb," and I asked him how to do it; I didn't know how to do my own move. And then he told me to go in the ring and take a Van Daminator, and I asked him, "From who?" My body's been through a helluva lot, as have a lot of the guys here. We have no off-season; we don't know what it is to have any down time; we don't take time off. We tape it up and hope for the best.

I DON'T USE SUPPLEMENTS. THE ONLY THING I USE RIGHT NOW IS PROTEIN POWDER AND PROTEIN BARS—ONLY BECAUSE THEY'RE VERY CONVENIENT FOR TRAVEL. I NEVER HAVE TRIED STEROIDS, BUT NO MATTER HOW MUCH I SAY THAT, NOBODY IS GONNA BELIEVE IT, SO I'VE GIVEN UP. I'VE BEEN ACCUSED OF TAKING ANABOLICS SINCE I WAS 16. AS A MATTER OF FACT, I HAD A URINALYSIS IN PREP SCHOOL BECAUSE I WENT FROM ABOUT 150 POUNDS TO 225 IN A MATTER OF LIKE SIX MONTHS. BUT I JUST HIT MY GROWTH SPURT. THEY DRUG-TESTED ME IN PREP SCHOOL, SO I'VE BEEN UNDER THAT MICROSCOPE FOR ABOUT 10 YEARS NOW. PEOPLE ARE GOING TO HAVE THEIR OPINIONS; I CAN'T CHANGE THEM. AS FAR AS THE ANABOLIC THING GOES, I'VE NEVER TRIED IT. BUT THEY WORK. BOTTOM LINE: THEY GET RESULTS. A LOT OF OUR BUSINESS IS BASED ON LOOK. YOU CAN BE ONE HELLUVA ATHLETE, BUT IF SOMEBODY TELLS YOU THAT YOU NEED MORE SIZE, A LOT OF PEOPLE WILL GO TO THAT QUICK FIX, BECAUSE THEY WANT THIS SO BAD. I HOPE WRESTLERS DON'T GET A BAD RAP, BECAUSE I'M WILLING TO SAY IT'S THE SAME THING THROUGHOUT PROFESSIONAL SPORTS. THERE'S ONLY ONE CIRCUS IN TOWN TO WORK FOR. IF YOU'RE A HOCKEY PLAYER, THERE'S ONLY ONE NHL; IF YOU'RE A BASKETBALL PLAYER, THERE'S ONLY ONE NBA. SOMETIMES YOU'RE WILLING TO SACRIFICE STUFF TO MAKE YOUR DREAM COME TRUE. I CAN'T BLAME THOSE GUYS AT ALL. BUT FOR ME, I'M IN THE SHAPE THAT I WANT TO BE IN RIGHT NOW. I'M HAPPY WITH THE WAY I WORK OUT; I'M HAPPY WITH MY DIET; I'M HAPPY WITH MY RESULTS. I DON'T NEED TO JEOPARDIZE MY HEALTH BY DOING ANABOLICS AND STUFF LIKE THAT.

John Cena

SOMETIMES IN my weight training, I'll do the Van Dam Lift. It's not part of my regular routine, but something that I do just for promotional purposes. The way it started, when I was a kid, I used to jump up in the air and do the splits and land on two benches with my legs — just to show off, no real purpose for it. While I was in that split position, I started picking up a dumbbell and holding it, which would make my muscles contract and allow me to pose and show off a pretty good physique. People would say, "Wow, that's really impressive!" Well, the weight got bigger the stronger I got, and I got encouraged to see if maybe I could get it officiated as a lift. Nobody else was doing it, and I got to where I thought that I could lift close to my weight. I talked to the Guinness people; I talked to Ripley's; and eventually I talked to the United States All-Around Weightlifting Association, which keeps track of lifts and presses that people don't normally do. They came to a gym to officiate my lift, and I did 166 1/2 pounds, the world record. To do it, you have to bend down while your legs are up on the bench, get the dumbbell off the ground — you've only got your groin to use for balance and leverage — pick that 166 1/2 pounds off the ground, and then lean back and pull the weight up. Nobody has challenged it, so I haven't had to beat it yet. But if someone challenged me right now, I could go in the gym and pull it off, no problem.

Van Dam lift

166.5

I'VE BEEN DOING A PRETTY INTENSE STRETCHING ROUTINE FOR ABOUT 15 YEARS, even before I became a professional wrestler. A lot of it was from being involved in martial arts classes as a kid, and I also really took an interest in health and physical education classes in high school. They start you out with stretching and jumping jacks; most kids hate doing it, but I liked it and really took to it. Jumping jacks are still a part of my routine. All the locker rooms that I've ever been in around the world, I'm always the only one that goes through this long of a stretching routine. It takes from 35 to 45 minutes, and I stretch every muscle in my body several times. I start standing on

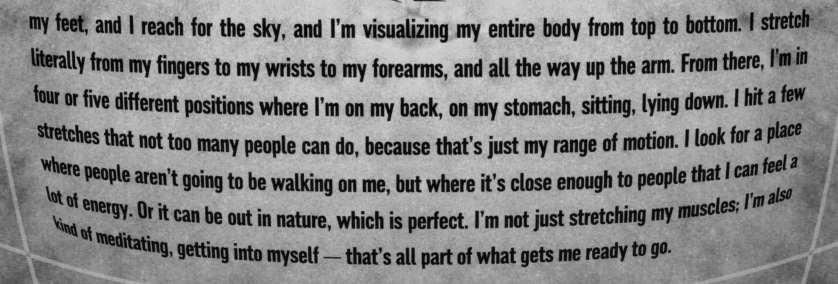

my feet, and I reach for the sky, and I'm visualizing my entire body from top to bottom. I stretch literally from my fingers to my wrists to my forearms, and all the way up the arm. From there, I'm in four or five different positions where I'm on my back, on my stomach, sitting, lying down. I hit a few stretches that not too many people can do, because that's just my range of motion. I look for a place where people aren't going to be walking on me, but where it's close enough to people that I can feel a lot of energy. Or it can be out in nature, which is perfect. I'm not just stretching my muscles; I'm also kind of meditating, getting into myself — that's all part of what gets me ready to go.

MORE THAN ANYTHING, I THINK I'VE LEARNED HOW TO WORK AROUND MY INJURIES THROUGH AMATEUR WRESTLING,
HOW TO TRAIN THROUGH THEM, HOW TO WRESTLE THROUGH THEM.

AT TIMES when most people would have to quit and not be able to perform, I'm able to do a little bit more. I know what to do and what not to do. Let's say I was an amateur wrestler in the Olympics, and I couldn't raise my arm over my head. I probably wouldn't wrestle, because that's real sport, real competition. In professional wrestling, we can work around that. I can do many things without lifting my arm. I can throw punches with my other arm, use it to whip him off the ropes, use it for a clothesline. You can work around whatever injury you have. If you have a sprained ankle, you just won't run; you'll stand right in the middle of the ring and bump the guy around and let him bump you around right there. If you have a broken arm, don't use that arm. I'll betcha 70 percent of the guys here right now have injuries, and they work around them — that's the beauty of sports entertainment. Guys get hurt more in this than in real sports. When you say it's all fake, sure, we know who the winner is gonna be, but I've still never had more injuries, and I played football for 12 years and wrestled for 20.

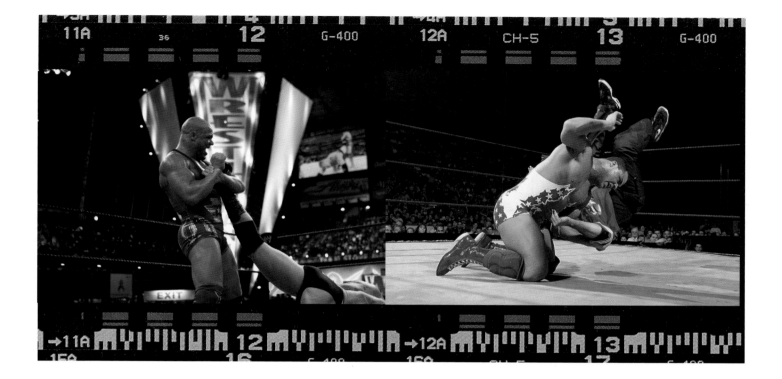

AMATEUR WRESTLING HAS MORE INJURIES THAN ANY OTHER SPORT, INCLUDING FOOTBALL,
AND I'VE BEEN HURT MORE IN THIS
THAN I WAS IN AMATEUR WRESTLING.

I'VE HAD neck surgery and knee surgery. A lot was wrong with my neck. I was fortunate to find a great doctor who does a method that no other doctor in the world does. His name is Dr. Jho, at Allegheny General Hospital in Pittsburgh. Dr. Jho read an article in the paper about me possibly retiring or having to have fusion, and he called and he told me, "Why don't you come down and have me take a look at you?" He could barely speak English — he's Korean. He basically looked at my MRI and said, "I can fix you." I thought the guy was full of shit, but I did further research, talked to a gymnast that he worked on — she was back in three and a half weeks, and she had a three-level problem; I had a two-level problem. Eight other wrestlers before me recently had neck injuries, whether it was spinal cord, disk problems, bone spurs, nerve damage or bruising of the spinal cord. Unfortunately, I had all five. Besides Stone Cold's, mine was probably the worst. What they usually do to fix it is fusion, but Dr. Jho doesn't believe in fusion. He believes that in order to be a fully effective wrestler and continue to have success, you need full flexibility and mobility in your neck. He decided just to repair my neck; any damage done, he would clip that off. He would make sure that the spinal cord was properly working, the nerves were flowing the right way. He would clip the bone spurs, even clip part of the disk that was sticking up against the spinal cord — I had two of them sticking up there. So I decided to go with the surgery, and two and a half weeks later my neck was better than before I injured it. These guys having fusion, what would take them a year to heal took me literally three weeks. The problem with fusion is, guys continue to get thrown on the back of their head, and that puts a lot more pressure on the other parts of the spinal cord because the fusion is so tight. You end up having to have more fusion.

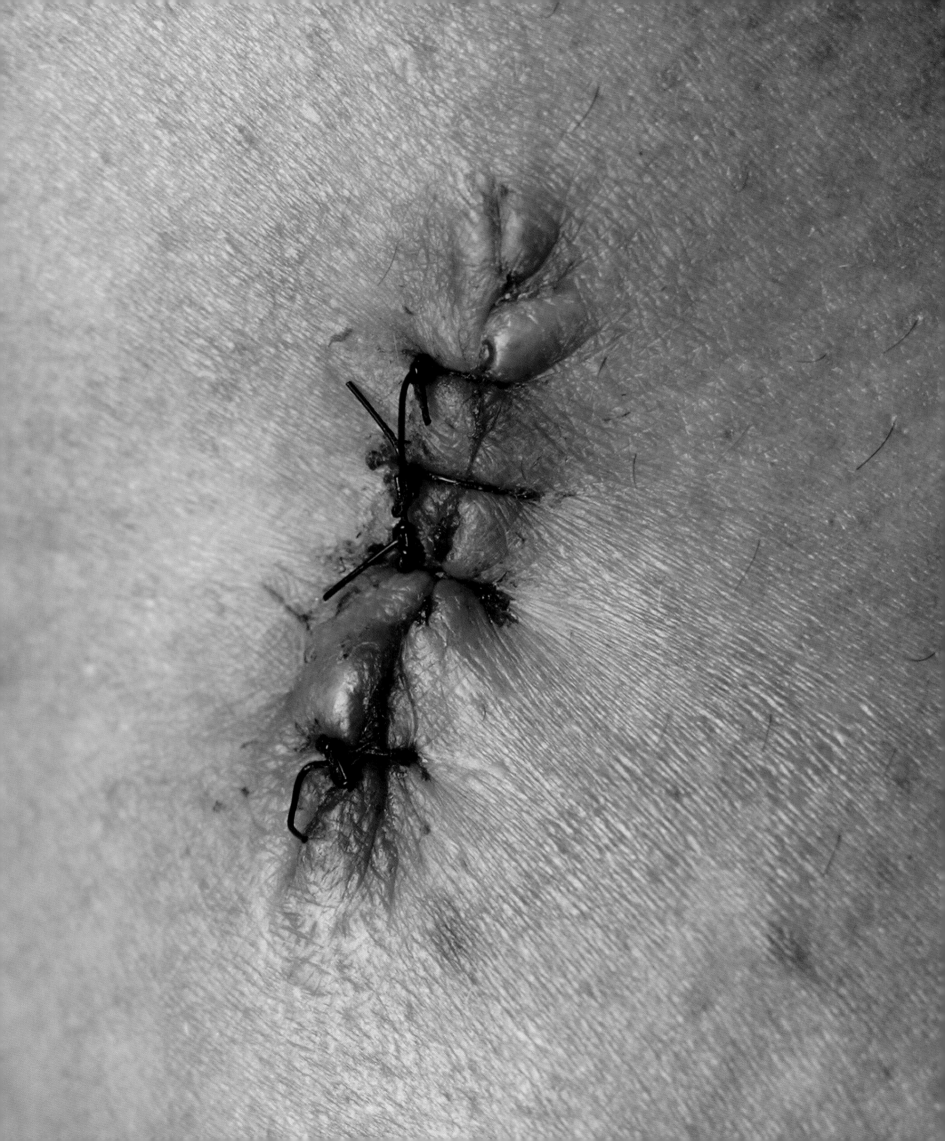

SECTION III

LIFE

The biggest fear I've had in the WWE

was the Tables, Ladders, and Chairs match at *SummerSlam* in 2000. I climbed up on a ladder with Jeff Hardy, and we were about 20 feet in the air, dangling on a rope, going for the tag team belts. The ladder was removed from underneath us, and we were dangling. Jeff kicked me, and I fell 20 feet to the ground on my back. As soon as I got kicked and I let go, I just automatically relaxed. I just waited to hear the bang from hitting the canvas. I came out of it unscathed, thank God. We went to war that night, and that match definitely put us on the map. And we all escaped injury-free, thank God.

I LET my daughter watch the show if I know that it's going to be a segment where I'm not doing something terribly sexual or something that she can't handle seeing. I'll know what the show's going to be, because I'm there, and I'll get on the phone and let them know back home what's OK and what's not OK for her to watch. For instance, when I was slammed through a table, I didn't mind her watching that. I sat with her, and I put a videotape in of it happening, and I watched it with her. That way, she knew Mommy was sitting right beside her, healthy and happy, that what she was seeing had already occurred, and Mommy was fine. However, other things, like when I had to wrestle in bras and panties, I just don't like her to see it.

But there's a certain amount that can't escape her, and I just try and explain it to her, like,

"PUNKIN, IF NICOLE KIDMAN, WHO'S A MOMMY, IS PLAYING A MURDERER ON TV, DOES THAT MAKE HER A MURDERER? NOOOO. WELL, MOMMY HAS A CHARACTER ON TV, AND THAT DOES NOT MEAN THAT THAT'S WHO MOM IS."

I want her to understand that Mom is just like any other character on TV. And Dad, too. Dad does some pretty wacky stuff. When he was electrocuted in the storyline, she was at his house. I called his wife and told her what was happening and said,

"DO NOT UNDER ANY CIRCUMSTANCES LET HER CATCH A GLIMPSE OF IT."

Even though Dad was coming home tomorrow, that's a visual that she didn't need to see.

I'D HAVE TO SAY MY WORST INJURY WAS THE DEAL WHERE I PUT MY RIGHT ARM THROUGH THE LIMOUSINE WINDOW DURING A WCW SHOW.

I GOT 199 STITCHES,

AND I CAME WITHIN A CENTIMETER OF CLIPPING MY NERVE. MY VIOLENCE TOOK OVER. IT WAS SUPPOSED TO BE SAFE, BUT ME WANTING TO BE THE BEST AND BE DIFFERENT, I TOOK IT TO A DIFFERENT LEVEL AND I PUT MYSELF IN A LOT OF JEOPARDY. BUT, HEY MAN, I JUST WANT TO ENTERTAIN THE PEOPLE — AND IT WAS GREAT TV. I WAS OUT ABOUT SIX MONTHS, I THINK — I CAN'T REALLY REMEMBER. THERE'S BEEN SO MANY FRIGGIN' INJURIES, THEY KINDA ALL RUN TOGETHER IN MY MIND. SOMETIMES MY NATURAL INSTINCTS TAKE OVER, AND I JUST GO OVERBOARD. IT'S THE HUNT, MAN; IT GETS THE ADRENALINE GOING. THEY HAVE TO KEEP A REIN ON ME, FOR DAMN SURE, THERE'S NO QUESTION ABOUT THAT. IF NOT, I'M MY OWN WORST ENEMY.

"PAIN IS GOOD, BUT EXTREME PAIN IS GREAT."

IT'S GOTTEN ME IN A LOT OF TROUBLE OVER THE PAST.

I HAVE AN EXTREMELY HIGH PAIN TOLERANCE AND THRESHOLD, AND I KINDA GET OFF ON IT, I DO.
NOT TO THE POINT OF THE DUDLEY BOYZ, BUT I DO GET OFF ON IT. WHEN I BLEED IN THE RING, IT FUELS MY FIRE.
WHEN I SEE BLOOD COMING OUT OF OTHERS, IT MAKES ME WANT TO DEVOUR THEM.
UNFORTUNATELY, PAIN IS A VERY BIG PART OF MY LIFE.

MY ROBES HAVE ALWAYS BEEN THE BEST AND THE MOST ELABORATE AND THE MOST EXPENSIVE. THEY WERE MADE BY A WOMAN NAMED OLIVIA WALKER, WHO LIVED IN ATLANTA. SHE'S PASSED AWAY. SHE MADE THE STUFF FOR THE RHINESTONE COWBOYS, FROM GLEN CAMPBELL TO DOLLY PARTON TO PORTER WAGNER, ALL OF THEM. I STARTED HAVING THEM MADE IN 1975. SHE MADE ME BETWEEN 25 AND 30 ROBES. I THINK THE FIRST ONE COST ME $3,200. THEY GOT MORE AND MORE LAVISH, AND THE PRICE WENT UP. I WAS PAYING $5,000 TO $6,000 FOR SOME OF THEM, A LOT OF MONEY FOR A ROBE BACK THEN. I'VE HAD AT LEAST SEVEN OF THEM STOLEN. AIRLINE WORKERS STOLE TWO OF THEM IN GERMANY. I LEFT TWO OF THEM AT A HOLIDAY INN IN BILOXI, MISSISSIPPI TO BE MAILED TO ME, BUT THEY DISAPPEARED. I HAD TWO AT WCW ON THE LAST DAY OF THE COMPANY, AND SOMEBODY STOLE THOSE. I GAVE ONE TO WCW TO PUT IN THEIR NITRO GRILL IN LAS VEGAS AND I NEVER GOT IT BACK. THAT WAS ONE OF MY BEST ONES. JULIE, THE GIRL FROM OUR COMPANY, MAKES THEM FOR ME NOW, AND THEY HAVE EVERY BIT THE CRAFTSMANSHIP THAT OLIVIA'S HAD. WHEN JULIE MAKES ONE, SHE HAS TO SHUT DOWN EVERYTHING ELSE FOR ABOUT THREE WEEKS TO DO IT. THEY REQUIRE THAT MUCH WORK.

MY FATHER DID NOT WANT ME IN THE BUSINESS.

HE DID EVERYTHING POSSIBLE TO KEEP ME OUT OF THE BUSINESS — AND I DID EVERYTHING POSSIBLE TO GET IN.

It was a cash business, and you used a lot of promoters, and my dad's philosophy was that as long as the promoters weren't stealing too much, he could put up with it. This guy in Bangor, Maine apparently was stealing too much for my dad's taste. So he said, "OK, it's Bangor, Maine — that's the spot you've got. If you can promote there, and promote successfully, fine. If that doesn't go, don't bother me ever again." He really wanted something for me that I didn't want. He wanted me to get a government job, be an attorney, be a professional, something with some security where I would have a, "pension". But those weren't my values at all. I think I was born to be a promoter; the risk-taking element is exciting. I have an extremely strong work ethic, much stronger than my dad's — that helps in an entrepreneurial environment.

MY DAD wanted to get out of the business, because he was really tired of it. I was scared to death that he was going to sell it to someone else, right out from underneath me. Essentially, I put together a bunch of mirrors — a little bit of money, but very little; it was almost all mirrors. My dad thought I had this, "angel", who was backing me, that it really wasn't my money. So I kinda hoodwinked him a little bit, but I had to because I didn't want him to sell the business to somebody else. I knew I couldn't work for anybody else — I'd tried that. It was a one-year deal for about a million bucks with specific dates for payments, and if we missed any of the payments, the stockholders kept all the money we'd paid them at that point and got the business back. It was a bit of a risk on our part. The only way that we could make it up was to expand and create a cash flow. But there was no way we were gonna be able to make it work strictly in the Northeast territory, not that I wanted to keep the business just in the Northeast anyhow. So we started expanding, and my dad didn't like it. Had he known we were gonna expand, he wouldn't have sold the business, because we were going into territories that belonged to his friends.

THIS SCAR I GOT ON THE BACK OF MY HEAD
WAS DELIVERED FROM VINCE MCMAHON HIMSELF WITH A STEEL CHAIR.

SO IF ANYBODY OUT THERE IS STILL WONDERING, "DO THE STEEL CHAIRS HURT?" — YES, THEY DO.
This was in St. Louis, and one of the guys, instead of stitching my head, put staples in.
I could have probably had a cleaner-looking scar than I do, but nonetheless that scar is courtesy of
Vince McMahon. I can't complain about it, because he's wearing several stitches from me also.
We've traded a few, and I'm kinda proud of it, actually.

THE LAST time I came back, one of the things I told Vince McMahon I'd like to do was help the young guys. With their promos, their delivery, their execution, how they say things, how they pause, how fast they talk, the intensity with which they talk, their mannerisms in the ring. These days, if you watch guys in the ring, they're all posing. Do you stand erect? Do you have presence? Do you pause a little bit? — of course, you do. But do you pose continuously and flex, and always look into the camera and play it? No, you don't. You have to know when to let the fans in — it's not every second of the match, which is what everybody is doing right now. The guys now don't know how to tell a story, and the business is moving 110 miles an hour. Guys aren't selling enough; and the workmanship within the ring, guys actually calling matches in the ring, that psychology has been lost. You've got a guy that's gonna send a guy into the ropes; the guy that's gonna get sent into the ropes is already running before the guy grabs his arm to send him into the ropes. Hey, that ain't right.

real weird feeling to walk down the ramp at a WWE event and be so ___arged by the crowd. It's an adrenaline rush that I can't compare to any- ___ve ever done. I can be hurt, so sore I can't even stand up straight, but ___y music hits and the crowd pops for me, it enables me to walk down ___p to the ring and do what I have to do. It is such a feeling to go out ___our your heart into it, and have a good match.

Then when I'm done and backstage again, it might take me an hour ___ minutes to shower, because I hurt. That's just part of the business. The m___ you do it, the more you're gonna hurt. You can't do this for over 200 days ___ and not pay a price. We're out there pounding our bodies. I've got lower ___ problems right now, three bulging discs, which really screws up my golf ___ and pisses me off.

___TER WE DO *SMACKDOWN!*, I'M LIKE A RUN-OVER SKUN___

___l bad and I look bad. It's like you were in the middle of a bunch of people that had bats, and everybody took a swing at ___

___come home, I walk through that door, I kiss my wife, I pet the dogs, and I head to the couch and sit down, and I don't want to do anything or say anything. I am ___ ___hile I'm on the road to be personable and to represent the company the best I know how, plus I'm expending so much energy in match after match. By the time I g___ ___ot much left; I'm all burnt up, just fried. I'm sick of looking at people; I'm sick of telling everybody how tall I am; I'm sick of answering questions about what I do ___ ___sick of hearing people say, "Damn, you're big." No shit, Sherlock. When I come home, I don't want to leave my home until I have to go back to work. And when ___ ___ rolls around, it's damn tough to go out that door and get back on the road.

YOU HURT IN SO MANY PLACES. AND IT'S NOT JUST ME; IT'S EVERYBODY. You look in the eyes of the other guys in the locker room and go, **"BROTHER, I KNOW WHAT YOU'RE GOING THROUGH."** That's why I think guys in wrestling are so close. We all know how fragile our careers are, and we're all looking out for each other.

Typically we leave Sunday night or Monday morning and we fly to the town that <u>Raw</u> is going to be in.

We have our first meeting of the day on the plane, PRETTY MUCH REWRITING THE SHOW.

Then we keep rewriting the show ALL DAY LONG.

On a typical <u>Raw</u> day, I'm up at six or seven, and I won't leave the arena that night until about midnight.

THERE'S NO DOWNTIME IN THERE; it's constant, on the go.

Then we go to the next town, sleep for a few hours, and get up and have a meeting for <u>SmackDown!</u>

Then we go to the arena, and the process STARTS ALL OVER AGAIN.

Wednesday, Thursday, and Friday, I'm in the office.

Saturday and Sunday, we have conference calls that usually go until about noon.

It's pretty much 24/7. But it's the nature of this business and I love it.
It's my passion and I wouldn't have it any other way.

I THINK YOU GET USED TO THE TRAVEL. FOR ME, IT'S IN MY BLOOD. WHEN I DON'T GO ON THE ROAD, IT BOTHERS ME. TO BE IN ONE PLACE FOR TOO LONG A PERIOD OF TIME, I START TO GO STIR-CRAZY. I'M SURE I COULD GET USED TO BEING AT HOME, BUT I'M NOT THERE YET.

Wrestlers have never had it as good as they do now. If they work full-time, they work four days a week. When guys are hurt, they get paid, and we pay their medical bills. We've put guys in drug and alcohol rehabilitation, paid for it, and paid their salaries. The McMahon family wants these kids to be healthy; it's smart business. Sure, the travel gets old, but it's a helluva lot easier now than it used to be.

GUYS TODAY HAVE NO IDEA OF THE PRESSURE THAT GUYS HAD ON THEM WHEN I GOT IN THE BUSINESS IN THE '70S. THERE WERE NO GUARANTEED CONTRACTS. YOU TRAVELED 1,500 TO 3,000 MILES A WEEK, THREE OR FOUR TO A CAR,

WITH CIGARETTE SMOKE, CIGAR SMOKE, AND 300-POUND WRESTLERS FARTING.

YOU SLEPT three to a room with two beds in an $8-a-night hotel, which I did hundreds of times. I slept on the damn floor; where do you think I slept? Do you think I was gonna sleep with a 300-pound, hairy wrestler and put a pillow between us? They gave me the bedspread to wrap myself in to sleep on the floor, and knowing what happens on bedspreads in cheap hotel rooms, I can't think of many people that would be excited that that would be their sanctuary for the night — but that's how it worked. If you got hurt, you went home and you hoped you'd stashed enough money in the cookie jar to be able to buy groceries and make your car payment. The office didn't take care of you, because you only got paid when you played, and there wasn't any worker's compensation. I get sick and tired of reading about ex-WWE wrestlers that have their 15 minutes with an Internet columnist or some obscure radio show, bitching about how demanding the business is, and the

pressure they have on them. The disgruntled guys that didn't make it for whatever reason were the ones that were eating Somas like they were M&Ms; were the ones that had to have their 6 or 12-pack at night; were the ones that had a girlfriend on the road. Wrestlers have to make good decisions outside the ring. I challenge anybody to tell me that if you have Wrestler X, who made a litany of bad decisions in his wrestling career, that individual would not have made comparable bad decisions if he were working for the Post Office or as a FedEx delivery man or a fast-food cook. Some people are not prepared to make good decisions, and it is our job in talent relations to cut those guys from the herd as quickly as we can. So I don't have a lot of empathy for disgruntled guys that leave here, saying, "The business did this to me." They're cowards; they need to look in the mirror and accept responsibility for their actions and grow up and be a man.

MY FIRST MATCH

WAS AGAINST NONE OTHER THAN THE HARDCORE LEGEND MICK FOLEY.
I WAS SO NERVOUS, BUT THE NERVOUSNESS ENDED QUICKLY AS I WAS
INTRODUCED TO AN IMMENSE AMOUNT OF PAIN AS WELL AS MR. SOCKO.

MY BIGGEST CHALLENGE

IT IS A VERY HUMBLING EXPERIENCE WHEN YOU ARE A FULL GROWN MAN AND
AGAINST YOUR WILL, YOU ARE THROWN AROUND LIKE A CHILD AND THERE IS
NOTHING YOU CAN DO ABOUT IT. BIG SHOW IS TRULY SUPER-HUMAN. THE
KEY TO COMPETING WITH BIG SHOW IS DON'T, BUT IF YOU ARE FORCED TO,
YOU HAD BEST GET CREATIVE.

MY MOST MEMORABLE MATCH

WAS COMPETING IN THE RING AT *WRESTLEMANIA X-SEVEN*. IMAGINE IF
YOU HAD THE OPPORTUNITY TO COMPETE IN THE BIGGEST SHOW IN THE
INDUSTRY, IN FRONT OF 67,925 LIVE IN ATTENDANCE AND MILLIONS
WATCHING AROUND THE WORLD AND YOU ARE FACING VINCE MCMAHON.
THE ICON OF OUR INDUSTRY, THE CREATOR OF THE VERY SHOW WE WERE
COMPETING IN, MY CREATOR, MY BEST MAN, MY FRIEND, MY BOSS, MY
DAD. I HAVE NEVER BEEN MORE PROUD TO BE IN A MATCH THAN I WAS
FOR THIS ONE. DAD, THANK YOU FOR ALWAYS GIVING ME OPPORTUNITIES
IN LIFE. I AM SO PROUD TO BE YOUR SON, I AM SO PROUD OF YOU AND I
LOVE YOU MORE THAN WORDS CAN EXPRESS.

MY GREATEST ACCOMPLISHMENT IN THE RING happened on June 24, 2001 at *King of the Ring*. That was the day that

I had the privilege of facing one of the greatest athletes in the world, Kurt Angle. The bond that Kurt and I created during that match is something that you can't describe it is just one of those unbelievable things in life that very few people get to experience. That match was 30 minutes of non stop adrenalin where we pushed each other to the absolute limit. I was so happy when he beat me because my body felt that I had been in several successive high speed car accidents. The pain subsided for us both for about a minute as everyone in the Meadowlands showed us their appreciation and bestowed upon us the highest honor that can be given, a standing ovation. For all that were there that night I would like to say thank you for giving us that magical moment and Kurt, you are the man!

THERE'S NOTHING LIKE THAT FEELING YOU GET WHEN YOU MAKE A STRONG, EMOTIONAL CONNECTION WITH A LIVE AUDIENCE. I HAVE A LOT OF FRIENDS NOW WHO ARE ACTORS THAT DON'T HAVE THE PRIVILEGE TO FEEL WHAT I HAVE FELT AND AM STILL ABLE TO FEEL WITH A LIVE AUDIENCE. I UNDERSTAND NOW WHY ACTORS GO BACK TO BROADWAY AND DO THEATER IF THEY GET THE CHANCE. IT'S FOR THAT CONNECTION WITH THE PEOPLE, THAT IMMEDIATE, SPONTANEOUS REACTION THEY ARE ABLE TO GET WITH THEIR PERFORMANCE. IT WASN'T THAT LONG AGO THAT I WAS WRESTLING IN A BARN. THERE WERE PROBABLY 100 PEOPLE IN THE CROWD, NO MORE THAN 150, BUT EVEN THEN, THE CONNECTION FELT SO GOOD THAT I CAN'T REALLY DESCRIBE IT.

When you're out there, you're so amped up, everything is intense and full throttle. And all of a sudden, it's like, "I got to go to bed in an hour?" — it doesn't work. Generally what I do, if I'm riding alone, which I do quite a bit just to give myself some me-time, is go for a bite to eat, then go to my room. I'll turn on *SportsCenter* and here in the States —and then I'll read. I like anything by John Grisham, Stephen King, and Chuck Palahniuk. Steven Brust wrote a book I really enjoyed, *To Reign In Hell*. Henry Rollins, who was the lead singer of Blackflag, has written journals that he calls the "Black Coffee Blues," which are chronicles of his life on the road. I'm kind of teaming up with Hulk Hogan to win the tag belts and then sitting at his house watching it with him on TV. Anything that I never envisioned I might get to do, I like to write down. That way, if I get too punchy, I can refresh my memory when I'm done wrestling. In addition to everything else, I'm a comic-book reader. If I have a pile I haven't

gotten to, I bring those with me on the road.

I also love to draw. I love drawing comic-book characters. On independent tours before I got to WWE, I would bring a sketchbook and a pencil with me on the road, and I'd draw. Then I'd go over everything with India ink, and it really jumped everything out. I had time for that on the indy circuit; on the tours, we might have a 24-hour drive, or be sleeping in a gym on blue mats. Instead of playing basketball in my free time, I'd just draw. But I didn't have the time to do it when I got to WWE.

Backstage, getting ready for a show, I kind of goof around. Some guys get real serious, but I love to joke around with everybody. You can't be too serious about this; you gotta remember that what we're doing is fun. I've always tried to take from what Owen Hart was like backstage; he was just so much fun to be around, always had a smile on his face. Kurt Angle is a lot the same way, a class act through and through. I'm getting to the point where I think I'm being looked at as a leader, and I don't want to be all surly and miserable. I'd rather have younger guys look at me and say, "OK, when I get to that position, that's who I want to try to be." But when it gets close to game-time, it's a coffee and thinking about what I'm gonna do out there. But the game eyes, or face, don't come on until that music hits. As soon as that happens, look out. As soon as I hear "You think you know me," get out of my way.

WRESTLING PRETTY MUCH CONSUMES MY THOUGHTS.

I'll go to bed thinking of ideas; I'll wake up thinking of ideas.

When I'm doing cardio, **I'M PICTURING IN MY MIND**

— just like when I was still a little kid — winning the world title.

I'll picture what I'll do when I win that, where it will be, how the crowd will react,

and me looking down and seeing my mom and Alanah in the front row.

Even while I'm watching a hockey game I'm thinking about wrestling;

it's always floating there in my mind.

**I THINK FOR THE PEOPLE THAT ARE REALLY
SUCCESSFUL IN THIS BUSINESS, THAT'S THE WAY IT IS.**

I'LL WRESTLE UNTIL IT'S NOT FUN ANYMORE. I'M NOT AN EXTREMELY YOUNG GUY, LIKE SOME OF THESE GUYS NOW WHO KNOW THEY'RE GOING TO BE HERE FOR ANOTHER 10 YEARS, SO I'VE HAD SOME THOUGHTS ABOUT WHAT I WANT TO DO. IT'S JUST A MATTER OF RESEARCHING AND FINDING OUT WHAT'S RIGHT FOR ME. CHANGE IS HARD FOR EVERYBODY. WHEN I THINK ABOUT BEING OUT OF THE BUSINESS, IT SCARES ME. I THINK THE THING THAT I'M GOING TO MISS THE MOST ARE SOME OF THE BONDS THAT I'VE MADE WITH PEOPLE. OUR LOCKER ROOM HAS REALLY CHANGED OVER THE YEARS TO WHERE NOW IT'S A GREAT GROUP OF GUYS THAT WE HAVE. I'LL MISS THAT, AND — I'M NOT GOING TO LIE — I'LL MISS GOING OUT THERE AND PERFORMING. THE PERFORMANCE ASPECT OF THIS IS THE MOST FUN. NO QUESTION, I'LL MISS GOING OUT IN THAT ARENA. AND I'LL MISS THE GUYS BACKSTAGE.

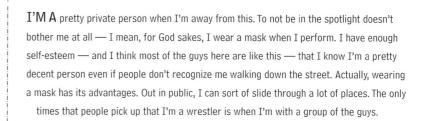

I'M A pretty private person when I'm away from this. To not be in the spotlight doesn't bother me at all — I mean, for God sakes, I wear a mask when I perform. I have enough self-esteem — and I think most of the guys here are like this — that I know I'm a pretty decent person even if people don't recognize me walking down the street. Actually, wearing a mask has its advantages. Out in public, I can sort of slide through a lot of places. The only times that people pick up that I'm a wrestler is when I'm with a group of the guys.

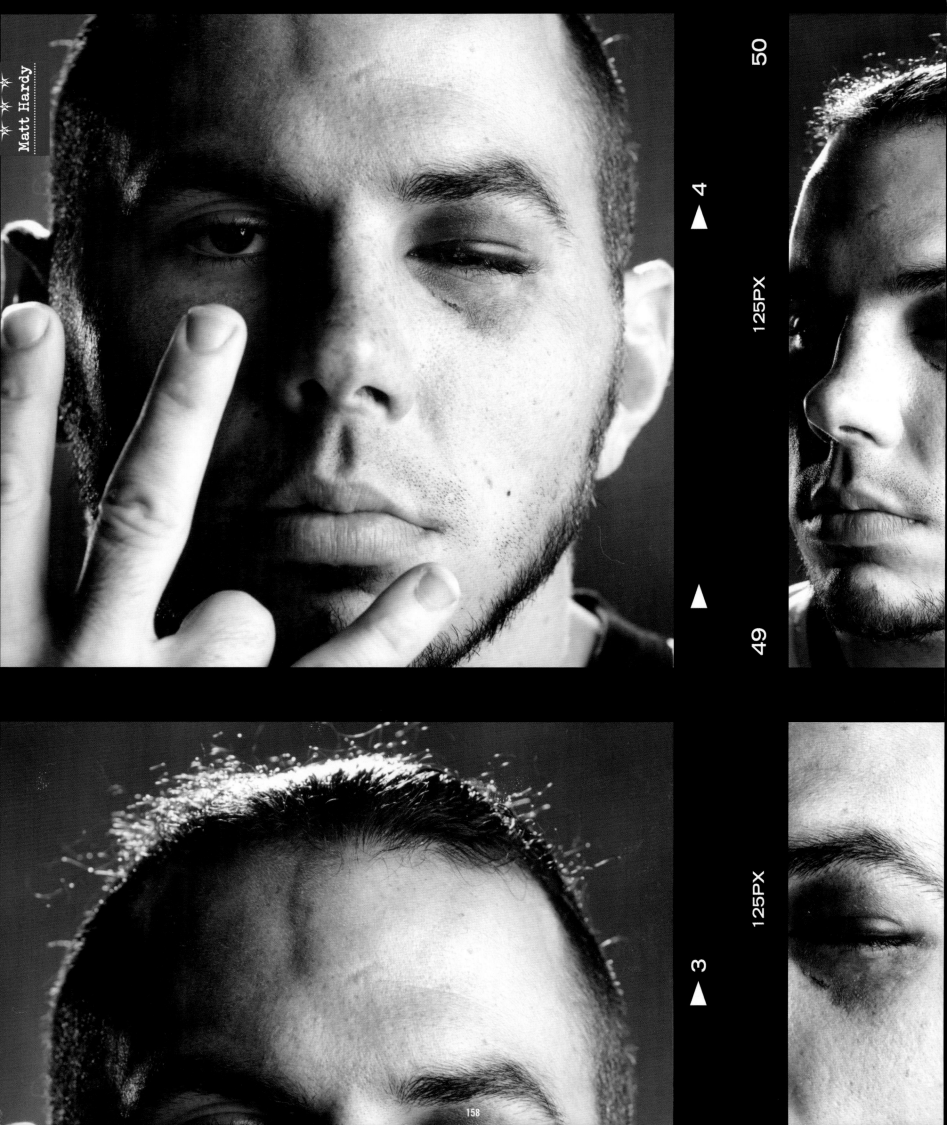

50

▲ 4

125PX

▲

49

125PX

▲ 3

WHEN AMY (LITA) AND I WERE ABLE TO TRAVEL TOGETHER, IT MADE THINGS SO EASY FOR US. BUT NOW THAT SHE'S BEEN OFF THE ROAD SO LONG, GETTING THROUGH HER NECK SURGERY, IT'S BEEN HARD. I KNOW SHE FELT SO ALONE BEING HOME BY HERSELF AND DEALING WITH THE REHAB; SHE WAS SO HAPPY WHEN WE'D COME HOME. SHE HAD A BIG MOUNTAIN TO CLIMB, AND I CAN TELL SHE'S COMING OVER THE HUMP NOW. NO WOMAN HAS EVER CAME BACK FROM AN INJURY THAT SERIOUS; I'M SURE SHE'LL BE THE FIRST ONE. SHE BROKE ALL THE TRENDS THE FIRST TIME SHE CAME INTO WRESTLING, AND SHE'LL DO IT AGAIN.

THE WAY WWE is structured, the talent will sign a contract that guarantees them a minimum amount of money. It's supposed to be a worse-case scenario amount of money, where if you get sick or hurt and you have to sit at home, you're gonna make something, hopefully enough for you to survive. After that, it's all incentive-based. If you work four or five times a week, you can double, triple, quadruple your money, whatever deal you have. You can also make more money for your merchandise sales and for being on Pay-Per-Views. The idea is, the harder you work and the more popular you get, the more money you can make.

The whole tradition of our business is to work hard. The only reason you don't work is if you physically can't. I've gone 4 years where I've been so hurt and beat-up, but I've worked through it. There's no union in wrestling, nobody to protect your interests except yourself.

That said, when you work yourself up to a certain level, the company will take care of you. I've got a knee injury. I tore my MCL; it pulled away from the bone partially. If it would totally pull away, that would weaken the ACL and the PCL, and then you might tear it all and you'd need full-blown surgery and be out for eight months. The company let me off of some house shows to rest my knee. But if this happened in my first six months here, I wouldn't be

getting a break like this. I would be working, keeping my fingers crossed that nothing happened to make my knee worse.

If you need medical attention or surgery for something that happened in the ring or was wrestling-related, the company is good about taking care of that. I've never known anyone that has been hurt that they left out to starve. But when you're on your personal time, it's on you. You're responsible for your health insurance. Think about that for a minute. You're selling insurance, and I walk in and I say, "Hey, would you mind selling me a policy? I jump off the top rope and land on my head for a living — but I probably won't get hurt." You can imagine how that goes over.

☆ TRIPLE-H'S ALL-TIME FAVORITE WRESTLERS ☆

THERE ARE SO MANY TO MENTION, AND I'M SURE I'M MISSING A LOT OF PEOPLE THAT I WOULD CONSIDER TO BE GREAT. I COULD GO ON ALL DAY ABOUT THE GREATS IN THE BUSINESS.

1. RIC FLAIR That's the guy I grew up loving and my dad grew up hating — we used to fight about that all the time. Flair was the consummate worker, always brought everybody to the next level, had the best matches. He had the entire package — the flamboyancy, the personality, the charisma, plus his unparalleled work ethic.

2. BUDDY ROGERS He was the predecessor to Flair, the guy that increased the speed of the business at the time. He was the kind of guy that could either make you love him or hate him by how he walked into the ring. I use a phrase on TV: "There's only one diamond in this business, and you're looking at him" — I stole that from Buddy Rogers. In late 2000, Vince McMahon started calling me BudRo; like I was today's Buddy Rogers. To me, that was the ultimate compliment.

3. RICKY STEAMBOAT I feel like Steamboat was the template for babyfaces in the business. Was always the good guy, had a great look, was athletic, could do anything, was a great worker, had charisma, had the personality. And Ricky Steamboat sold like nobody else.

4. SHAWN MICHAELS To me, Shawn is today's version of Steamboat. I think Shawn prefers to be a heel, but I thought he was best as a babyface. He sells like nobody else. Probably the best pure athlete I've ever seen in the business. Shawn can do anything. As a testament to that, he was off for five years with a back injury, and in his first match back, we wrestled at *SummerSlam* and had one of the great matches of my career.

5. RAY STEVENS He was an incredible worker, and a fantastic storyteller. He also increased the speed of the business. Ray was big in a lot of territories, but a lot of people don't know about him because he never had major stints until very late in his career with WWE.

TRIPLE H HOLDING A PICTURE OF BUDDY ROGERS.

6. NICK BOCKWINKEL He always looked immaculate, wrestled immaculately, and told unbelievably good stories. Everything he did was right-on; there was never anything see-through in anything he did. Nick would go 30 minutes, and everything just built for that 30 minutes; he'd go 60 minutes, and it would build for that 60 minutes — and the end would just blow your mind.

7. PAT PATTERSON Pat was very much in the vein of Ray Stevens — incredible psychology, got the most out of everything he did. I have an affinity for Pat, too, because I work with him on a regular basis and I consider him to be one of the smartest guys in the business.

8. DORY FUNK Dory was a very dry personality and was kinda one speed, but he was so believable that you bought into everything that he did. He was an incredible technician. He didn't look like much and wasn't flamboyant, but, boy, when he turned it on, you knew it was on.

9. SUPERSTAR BILLY GRAHAM He set the template for today's personalities. Hulk Hogan, to me, is a cheap Superstar Billy Graham knockoff. The lingo, the look, the flexing of the 25-inch pythons, the whole deal — Superstar was doing that way before Hulk Hogan. Superstar might not have been the greatest worker in the world, but from a personality standpoint and for his impact on the business, I give him a lot of credit.

10. ARN ANDERSON This may be a controversial pick, but it isn't to me. I feel that Arn was one of the most underrated guys in the business. He was a great constant; never wavered, never faltered, had great matches with everybody. You couldn't see through anything he did, and he cut some of the best promos ever in the business. His promos were believable, intelligent, scathing, cutting-edge stuff.

☆ HONORABLE MENTION ☆

TULLY BLANCHARD — An incredible worker. **DUSTY RHODES** — For sheer personality and charisma. **BOB ORTON JR.** — A tremendous performer.

HARLEY RACE — Unbelievable technician and great psychologist. **PAUL ORNDORFF** — Great technician. **RICKY MORTON** — As a babyface, he was unbelievably good.

BOBBY EATON — For his high flying, and combining that with storytelling and psychology. **STEVE AUSTIN** — A guy who took charisma and personality to a whole new level.

FREDDIE BLASSIE — Ahead of his time in doing things for shock value. They say he actually gave people heart attacks. **MAGNIFICENT MURACO** — Tremendous performer.

WHEN I CAME HERE, I WAS EXPECTING THAT THEY WOULD TELL ME THAT THEY WANTED ME TO GET BREAST IMPLANTS. BUT THAT REALLY WASN'T TOUCHED ON AT ALL. IT WAS ALL ABOUT, "WE LIKE THE WAY YOU ARE." THEN A COUPLE MONTHS LATER, AFTER THE FIRST DIVA PHOTO SHOOT, JIM ROSS PULLED ME IN AND HE TOLD ME THAT THEY DID NOT WANT ME TO GET BREAST IMPLANTS. THEY SAID IF I WOULD LIKE TO GET BREAST IMPLANTS FOR MY OWN REASONS, THAT'S FINE, AND, OF COURSE, LET THEM KNOW. BUT THEY WANTED TO REITERATE THE FACT THAT, "WE LIKE YOU THE WAY YOU ARE; YOU DON'T NEED TO GET THOSE TO GET AHEAD IN THIS BUSINESS, TO MAKE MORE MONEY IN THIS BUSINESS. YOU BRING OTHER THINGS TO THE TABLE." THAT WAS A BIG RELIEF FOR ME, BECAUSE IF THAT WERE SOMETHING THAT I HAD DONE, IT WOULD BE IMPORTANT TO ME THAT I WAS DOING IT FOR ME, NOT SOMEBODY ELSE. ONE OF THE COMMENTS I ALWAYS GET IS, "DON'T GET BREAST IMPLANTS, BECAUSE YOU WILL JUST LOOK LIKE EVERY OTHER ONE OF THOSE GIRLS — NOT JUST THE GIRLS HERE, GIRLS EVERYWHERE." I FIT MORE OF THAT MODEL, STATUESQUE FIGURE. I SOMETIMES TRY TO THINK OF WHAT I WOULD LOOK LIKE WITH BIGGER BOOBS; I WOULDN'T KNOW WHAT TO DO WITH THEM; I WOULDN'T KNOW HOW TO ACT.

I DEFINITELY THINK THIS BUSINESS IS TOUGHER FOR WOMEN THAN MEN.

IT'S A BUSINESS THAT'S DOMINATED BY MEN. IN SOME WAYS, YOU COULD SAY WOMEN ARE THE LUCKY ONES BECAUSE THERE'S ONLY A HANDFUL OF US AND WE'RE USED A LOT ON TV. BUT IT'S HARD TO FIT IN WITH THE GUYS, EVEN THOUGH I REALLY DO FEEL LIKE PART OF THE FAMILY NOW. IT'S A BUNCH OF GUYS BACKSTAGE JUST BEING GUYS.

FOR ME, GETTING READY FOR A MATCH IS AN ALL-DAY THING, BECAUSE I'M NOT AS GOOD AS THE GUYS IN THE RING;

I'm still learning. Fit Finley, who's a godsend to all of us female wrestlers, works with us from the time the ring is up. Usually from around three o'clock in the afternoon until the doors open, we're in the ring, learning new moves if we have to put something new into the match, putting the match together, going over a match, over and over and over. It's a really stressful period for me. I really want to prove myself in the ring. I know people don't expect a lot from me, so I want to surprise them, even if it's one little spot in a match.

I WANT THEM TO GO, "WHOA! GEE, SHE'S GETTING GOOD."

Before I go out for the match, I need to be alone in a corner and breathe deep and calm myself down, and go over what I'm going to do in the ring. I tend to get really, really nervous and hyper. I just have to make sure I keep my breathing under control and relax myself, try to remind myself over and over that if I mess up the crowd's not going to know, unless I do something really ridiculous.

EDGE FIXED HIMSELF UP WITH MY SISTER ALANAH. HE CAME UP TO ME ONE DAY AND SAID,

"I NEED TO TALK TO YOU."

AND HE PULLED ME ASIDE AND HE SAID,

"I DON'T KNOW HOW YOU'RE GOING TO HANDLE THIS, BUT I WANT YOU TO KNOW THAT I'D LIKE TO DATE YOUR SISTER, AND I JUST WANT YOUR PERMISSION."

AND I WENT,

"YOU WHAT?"

And they dated and eventually got married, and I think it's a great relationship they've got. I like Edge; he's a great guy. I remember when I first broke into the business, my first match was his second match, at a small arena in Toronto. Then we went our separate ways, and we met back up at the exact same time in WWE. My sister is really into fitness, so it's great for him, because he always needs a little extra push when it comes to working out.

Val Venis
SEAN MORLEY

THE BIGGEST SCARE I HAD WAS WHEN EDGE AND I WERE WRESTLING TOGETHER AS THE CONQUISTADORES UNDER THE MASKS.

I BIT A DIVE ON THE FLOOR ON JEFF HARDY AND LANDED ON THE SIDE OF MY HEAD AND FELT A SHOCK GO ALL THE WAY UP MY SIDE, AND MY RIGHT ARM WENT COMPLETELY NUMB. WHEN I GOT UP, MY ARM WAS HANGING THERE LIKE A WET NOODLE. IT TOOK ME A GOOD COUPLE MINUTES JUST TO GET SOME TINGLING BACK IN MY ARM. IT WAS BIG SCARE. IT'S WEIRD, BECAUSE YOU'RE OUT THERE IN FRONT OF THE CROWD AND YOUR ADRENALINE IS PUMPING, AND THE FIRST THING THAT CROSSED MY MIND WAS, "I HAVE TO FINISH THIS MATCH. HOW AM I GOING TO GET THROUGH THIS MATCH?" BECAUSE WE WERE ON PAY-PER-VIEW. LUCKILY THERE WAS ONLY FOUR OR FIVE MINUTES LEFT IN THE MATCH, AND WE GOT THROUGH IT. WHEN I CAME BACK THROUGH THE CURTAIN, THAT'S WHEN THE FEAR SET IN. LUCKILY, IT WAS JUST A PINCHED NERVE; I HAD A BIT OF A STINGER THAT CAUSED THE ARM TO GO NUMB.

WRESTLERS ARE A DIFFERENT BREED. IF YOU GET HURT IN THE RING, NOT FINISHING YOUR MATCH IS NOT AN OPTION, UNLESS YOU'RE UNCONSCIOUS. IT'S ALL ABOUT PERFORMING AND GIVING THE FANS EVERYTHING THAT YOU HAVE. THE MATCH IS ALWAYS FIRST. YOU'RE OUT THERE IN FRONT OF A LOT OF FANS, AND MILLIONS MORE ARE WATCHING ON TV, SO YOU'VE GOT A JOB TO DO, AND YOU'VE GOT TO DO THAT FIRST AND WORRY ABOUT YOURSELF SECOND. PLUS, I THINK OUR THRESHOLD FOR PAIN IS A LITTLE HIGHER THAN THE AVERAGE PERSON'S. WE PUT OUR BODIES ON THE LINE FOUR OR FIVE NIGHTS A WEEK, SO OUR BODIES SEEM TO BUILD UP SOME KIND OF TOLERANCE FOR PAIN.

IT IS A VERY CONSUMING BUSINESS.
I THINK FOR VINCE, IT IS HIS VOCATION AND HIS AVOCATION,
HIS HOBBY AND HIS LOVE
— HE THOROUGHLY, THOROUGHLY ENJOYS DOING IT.

I think we both have the philosophy that we'd like to do it as long as it's fun, as long as we feel like we're contributing, and as long as it's the right thing to do. We're smart enough to look at it and say, "You know what? Somebody else could be doing this better. Let's move aside." And Shane and Stephanie are certainly coming along in those roles.

I'M A 54-YEAR-OLD FEMALE, AND CLEARLY THIS IS A VERY MALE-DOMINATED TV SHOW. SO, YES, THERE ARE A LOT OF THINGS ON OUR SHOW THAT SOMETIMES MAKE ME UNCOMFORTABLE - BUT THEY'RE SUPPOSED TO. THERE ARE FEMALES MY AGE THAT WATCH OUR SHOW, SO A LOT OF TIMES I AM LIKE A BAROMETER FOR THE SHOWS. QUITE OFTEN, I AM WATCHING AND SEEING THE STORYLINE UNFOLD ALONG WITH EVERYBODY ELSE, UNLESS I AM INVOLVED IN IT. I LIKE TO WATCH AND BE SURPRISED.

tions, like "Wow! This guy's right out there; he's talking about souls, about things that people don't like to talk about." Initially, people were terrified of me. Kids in the arena would be bawling when I made my ring entrance. It was like the boogeyman had come to life. And somewhere in the process of that first year, year and a half, the fans really got high on that character; it became a really cool character. I think just by my size, and the way this character looked, and he moved so slow, and then there was this sudden burst, this explosion of energy, and then he'd be right back to slow again — the whole package just fascinated people. It was just one of those rarities when everything fell into place and just hit. For me, it was stuff that I was interested in anyway, so that made it easy. I lived the character, lived it for all those years. I always was in black, going to the airport, going to the gym, everywhere. When Sara and I met, my whole wardrobe was black. She's actually responsible for getting me to wear stuff that's not black.

PEOPLE ARE BECOMING MORE SOPHISTICATED, MORE BLOODTHIRSTY,

It will be interesting to see where all this is going to end up.

People have preconceived ideas about what wrestling is. What disturbs me is that some of these ideas defy logic. You can actually see somebody get picked up and thrown down, and yet somehow it didn't really happen; it was a camera angle, or the guy knew how to fall. Where the confusion comes in is that the outcome is predetermined, but how you get to that outcome is real, very real, more real now than ever before. I'm curious whether in another 10, 15 years, wrestling will be more of an Ultimate Fighting Challenge-type thing; that's kind of where the business is progressing.

I HAD A LITTLE PROBLEM
AT *WRESTLEMANIA.*

ME AND KURT ANGLE WERE WRESTLING, AND I EXECUTED A SHOOTING STAR PRESS. IT'S A MOVE WHERE I GET ON THE TOP ROPE AND DO A BACKFLIP INTO THE RING. IT'S A HARD MOVE, BUT IT'S SOMETHING THAT I'D BEEN DOING FOR A LONG TIME OFF THE DIVING BOARD INTO THE POOL.

I was saving it for something special, like <u>WrestleMania</u>. Millions of people are watching. I thought I'd bring it out of the repertoire...once.

But I slipped on the rope. The ropes were a little slick; we were the 12th match of the night. They were wiped down before we went out, but when I crawled up there, I put my hand on the rope - of course, I was very sweaty - and when I went to execute the jump, my right foot slipped a little bit, so I tried to reposition and go at the same time. I tuck my feet, then I jump into the ring and do a gainer. As I came around in my flip, I still thought I was gonna execute the move,

but I landed right on my face. I tried to stop and protect myself, but couldn't. Kurt, luckily enough, moved out of the way just in time.

I WAS a good 10, 12 feet off the mat on my jump, and I landed smack on my forehead and my face. I weigh 290 pounds, so you can just image the force and the momentum of that. When I hit, I don't remember anything because I got a concussion. I won the match, but I couldn't tell you what happened. Kurt covered me after the spill I took, and he pulled me up to my feet, and I ended up F-5ing him. I don't know if it was just instincts taking over or what; I don't know what was going through my head.

After the match, from what people have told me, I didn't want to leave the ring. I was a bear with them trying to get me out of the ring. They were trying to get me onto the stretcher, but I have a phobia of stretchers, and I have a phobia of ambulances and hospitals. I guess all that was embedded in my head, and I just wasn't having any of it. Finally, when they got me to the hospital about an hour and a half later, I had a CAT scan and a skeletal check to make sure nothing was broken, and nothing was. I just had a pretty severe concussion. When I was sitting in the emergency room and coming to and realizing what could have happened and how I could be sitting in a wheelchair or even worse than that, I felt very lucky. My thick head and my thick neck really saved my ass. I owe it all to amateur wrestling, and all the years I built my neck up.

I WANTED TO GET INTO WRESTLING THE DAY I FIRST SAW IT. MY DAD IS ONE OF THE ALL-TIME FAMOUS WRESTLERS,

DUSTY RHODES, "THE AMERICAN DREAM"

I go back to Florida Championship Wrestling, watching Dad. My earliest memory that sticks out was Dad wrestling The Spoiler in the Eddie Graham Sports Arena in Orlando. It was just awesome; I'd never seen anything as cool as that.

THE WRESTLING, IT'S IN MY BLOOD, IN MY VEINS. I JUST LOVE IT. IT'S NOT A MONEY THING;

YOU HAVE TO HAVE IT IN YOUR HEART AND SOUL.

There's plenty of people out there right now that have been in the business 10 years that still don't know what the hell they're doing, and it's frustrating for me as a fan and as an entertainer to look at that. I think, "You don't have the heart for this." I do. I have the heart and soul, and the want and desire to do this, no matter if I was doing it for a charity event or what. The money's nice, but it's more than that. This is just something that I always wanted to do.

THERE WERE a few black wrestlers around, but none really on top, none really working in the position where the Hogans were, guys like that. We always had our Junkyard Dogs, our Tony Atlases, but they never really broke the barrier of just medium, mid-card guys. But I always felt like there was an opportunity for me. You're always gonna come up on barriers in front of you; you've just got to figure your way around them. When I went to wrestling school, I realized something really, really quick: I was better than most of the guys I was working with; actually, I was better than all of the guys that I was training with. And I'd watch wrestling on television and say, "I know I'm better than that guy" or "I could compete with that guy." I always felt really, really confident in my talent, and I was always really comfortable being in front of a crowd. This is entertainment, and I've been an entertainer throughout my life. I was always the class clown, always the one in the family making everybody laugh, always the one impersonating someone, quoting lines from movies, stuff like that. Entertaining was just something that was natural for me. So I knew from the day I first got in a wrestling ring that I was going to be in the big company one day. I was in it two years and about six months before I quit my job and was just a full-time wrestler.

MOST OF THE GUYS THAT COME IN NOW ARE PRETTY JACKED-UP, PRETTY MUSCLED-UP.

But I realized a long time ago that's really not what's going to make you successful in this business. That's not what's gonna put you on top. In-ring performance and looking good has a lot to do with it,

BUT IF YOU CAN'T CARRY THE OTHER SIDE, YOU'RE JUST SPINNING YOUR WHEELS.

Most of the guys working the main event aren't guys that go flying around, aren't guys that look like Arnold Schwarzenegger. Most of the guys that work on top are guys, just like myself,

that go out there and just thrill the crowd, and want to rag-tag somebody and beat somebody up.

Guys coming into the business nowadays, their bodies are all jacked-up and pumped-up; they look like bodybuilders. It's more dangerous for those guys. I can go out there and let those guys slam me around all day, and I'm gonna be OK. But if they get slammed the wrong way, something's gonna pop. Brock Lesnar is OK, because he's got the size to carry what he carries, and he's pretty athletic, and he's been wrestling for years. But that Batista — he's just freaky, too big. Being like that, you can't go out and perform at a high rate; something's gonna happen, something's gonna give.

And that's what happened. He was pie-facing a guy and tore his triceps, tore it right off the bone. I've never been pumped-up or all muscled-up like that, and my body has held up for me pretty good. What those kids don't realize is that once you start looking a certain way, you can't stop looking that way. Once you build your character to look a certain way, the fans will not accept you any other way. You can't go out there if you haven't been working out in the gym all week. I can go for a week without working out and come into the ring, and fans will accept me because they don't expect me to be all jacked-up.

SOME PEOPLE WOULD MAKE THE ARGUMENT THAT SINCE I'VE COME BACK, I HAVEN'T BACKED OFF MUCH IN WHAT I DO IN THE RING. BUT I HAVE A LITTLE BIT, AND I PLAN ON BACKING OFF EVEN MORE. WHEN YOU'VE BEEN AROUND A LONG TIME AND ARE POPULAR WITH THE FANS, THEY ALLOW YOU, WHETHER CONSCIOUSLY OR NOT, TO DO LESS. YOU GIVE THEM YOUR TRADEMARK STUFF, BUT DON'T HAVE TO DO ANYTHING CRAZY, AND THEY STILL GO AWAY HAPPY. THAT'S BEEN A LEARNING PROCESS FOR ME, BECAUSE IT USED TO NOT MATTER TO ME WHAT RISKS I TOOK IN THE RING. I WAS ALWAYS HURTING TO SOME EXTENT, BUT NEVER REALLY CARED ABOUT IT. NOW, I DO CARE, BECAUSE I HAVE A REASON TO BE HEALTHY. I WANT TO BE ABLE TO CHASE

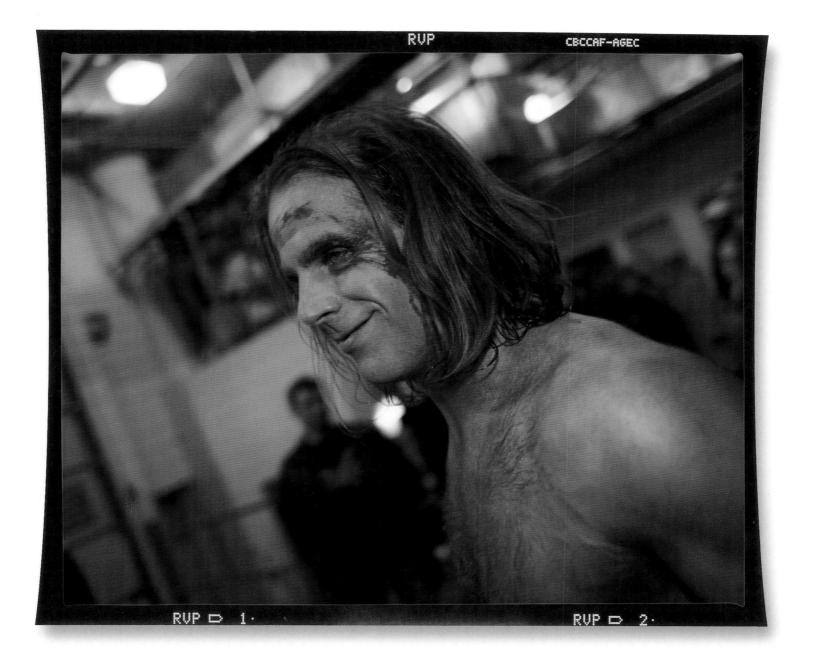

MY SON AROUND THE YARD; I WANT TO BE ABLE TO CHASE MY WIFE AROUND THE HOUSE. PHYSICALLY, I CAN STILL DO THE HIGH-RISK STUFF, BUT YOU'RE NOT GOING TO SEE A LOT OF IT FROM ME. I USED TO WONDER, "WHY DO GUYS STAY AROUND FOR SO LONG?" AND NOW I KNOW WHY. BECAUSE WHEN YOU HAVE A FAMILY, YOU CAN NEVER EARN ENOUGH, BECAUSE YOU WANT TO GIVE THEM EVERYTHING YOU CAN. I'M GOING TO STAY AROUND UNTIL SOMEBODY KICKS ME OUT THE DOOR. AS LONG AS THEY'RE WILLING TO ALLOW ME TO WORK, I'M GOING TO WORK, AT LEAST UNTIL I DON'T ENJOY IT OR I FEEL THAT GOD WANTS ME DOING SOMETHING ELSE. I WANT TO BE ABLE TO PROVIDE AS MUCH AS I CAN FOR MY WIFE AND MY SON.

WHEN YOU'VE GOT AN 80-YEAR-OLD WOMAN LIKE MAE YOUNG
WHO YOU'RE SUPPOSED TO PUT THROUGH A TABLE,
AT FIRST YOU GO, "WHAT?"
BUT WHEN SHE COMES UP TO YOU AND SLAPS YOU IN THE FACE AND TELLS YOU,
"DON'T BE A WUSS WITH ME; THROW ME THROUGH; I WANNA GO THROUGH"
— WHAT ARE YOU GONNA DO? BY FAR, THAT WAS THE TOUGHEST PERSON, POUND FOR POUND, WE'VE EVER BEEN IN THE RING WITH.

D-VON DUDLEY

MAE YOUNG is about 80 years old, but she is without a doubt the toughest woman I have ever met in my life, and probably tougher than half the men in the wrestling business. She was so happy and excited to work with me and D-Von. The first thing that we did to her in the ring was the "Wassup" spot — D-Von dove into an 80-year-old woman's crotch. To have a big, black head in an 80-year-old woman's crotch, that in itself is hysterical. Next thing we did was Superbomb her off the top rope through a table — she loved it. When I slammed Mae Young to the mat before we gave her the "Wassup" diving headbutt spot, I was very ginger with her. I picked her up very lightly, put her down very gently. After the match was over and we'd gone to the back, she came up to me, grabbed me by the wrist like only Lou Thesz could have done, "Listen, hotshot, if you're gonna slam me, slam me like one of the boys." You could imagine the look on my face, seeing this little, blonde lady telling me that. From there, we did the spot where I Superbombed her off the top of the stage, 12 feet from the ground, through two tables. She has since suggested to me on three different occasions that we do the same spot from the top of the steel stage.

Taking an 80-year-old woman and throwing her off the stage, yeah, if you take it for face value, it's awful. But this is entertainment. People know it's entertainment; we tell them it's entertainment. The whole idea was to make the Dudley Boyz more dastardly bad guys. But you tell me what is more sick: The Dudley Boyz doing that to a woman to become dastardly bad guys in the fans' eyes, or the fans cheering and applauding the Dudley Boyz for doing it and making us the biggest babyfaces in WWE? I'll never forget having Mae Young in my arms before I dropped her off the stage and through the tables, and looking out and seeing people screaming and chanting with their hands in the air, "Yeah, do it! Kill her!" This is what the people want. We give them what they want the safest way we know how.

THE "STINK FACE" WAS BORN IN MOBILE, ALABAMA.

I had a match there versus Big Bossman. I clotheslined Bossman in the corner, and he fell flat on his butt. I heard this one lady yell out, "Rikishi, stick your butt in his face!" I turned around and looked for the lady — that's how the, "Stop, turn around" part of it came about. As I stood there, I thought, "Well, let me try this." As I went over to Bossman to do it, the closer I got to him, the louder the crowd started to roar. And when I turned around to stick my butt in his face, it got the biggest reaction I'd ever had in wrestling. I thought, "My goodness! I've been looking all this time for something that would give me a pop like this, and it's been right behind me all the time."

After that, I brought the Stink Face to TV with me, and it's been my biggest payoff. I can do some impressive things in the ring for a person my size, but it's a lot easier getting a pop from the crowd by sticking my butt in someone's face. I can get a lot more mileage out of doing the Stink Face than I can doing a splash off the steel cage, and it's a lot safer — at least for me; I don't know if it is for the guy that's taking it.

A LOT OF PEOPLE ASK ME WHAT I WANT TO DO WHEN I'M DONE WITH THIS. I DON'T EVER WANT TO BE DONE WITH THIS. I'VE PUT ALL MY CHIPS IN THIS. I WANT TO DO THIS AS LONG AS I CAN. IF I CAN NO LONGER PHYSICALLY FUNCTION IN THE RING, I WOULD LOVE TO SIT AT THE COMMENTARY TABLE AND ANNOUNCE THE MATCHES. I'D FRIGGIN' RING THE BELL; I'D BE A REF; I'D BE IN THE BACK DOING WHATEVER I COULD. I'LL HOLD A CAMERA; I'LL PUT THE FRIGGIN' RING UP. I LOVE THIS ATMOSPHERE. THIS IS SUCH A TIGHT-KNIT GROUP, AND THIS IS SUCH A GREAT COMPANY TO WORK FOR. I FELL IN LOVE WITH WRESTLING WHEN I WAS A KID, AND NOW THAT I'M HERE IN WWE, I'VE FALLEN IN LOVE WITH THIS WHOLE BIG SHOW, THIS BIG CIRCUS. I WANT TO BE PART OF THIS, WHETHER I'M THE BEARDED LADY OR WHETHER I'M THE GUY TAKING TICKETS, I DON'T CARE.

I JUST WANT TO DO THIS UNTIL I CAN'T

EVEN MOVE

PEOPLE ASK ME WHAT IT'S LIKE TO STAND IN THE PYRO WHEN I COME OUT ONSTAGE.

IT FRIGGIN' HURTS!

ACTUALLY, IT'S A LOT OF FUN, BUT IT CAN'T BE REAL GOOD FOR MY HEALTH. WHEN I FIRST STARTED DOING IT, I SINGED ALL THE HAIR ON MY BODY — THAT'S WHY I NOW SHAVE MY BODY AS CLOSELY AS I CAN. I GET HOLES BURNED IN MY KNEEPADS AND TRUNKS. THE ONLY THING IT HASN'T GOTTEN IS MY GOATEE, WHICH I'M VERY SURPRISED ABOUT. I POUR A COUPLE BOTTLES OF WATER ON MYSELF BEFORE I GO OUT, AND THAT HELPS SOME.

AS LONG AS IT LOOKS GOOD AND IT DOESN'T KILL ME, I'LL KEEP DOING IT.

TRIPLE H AND SHAWN MICHAELS REMIND ME OF A GUY I KNEW A LONG TIME AGO — ME. THEY LIVE AND BREATHE IT, TRIPLE H ESPECIALLY.

TRIPLE H IS THE BEST PERFORMER IN OUR BUSINESS.

HE'S GOT A PASSION FOR IT, AND HE'S LEARNED HOW TO DEAL WITH THE ADVERSITY. HE JUST WANTS TO BE THE BEST, AND HE JUST WANTS TO BE OUT THERE EVERY NIGHT — AND THAT'S HOW YOU GET TO BE THE BEST.

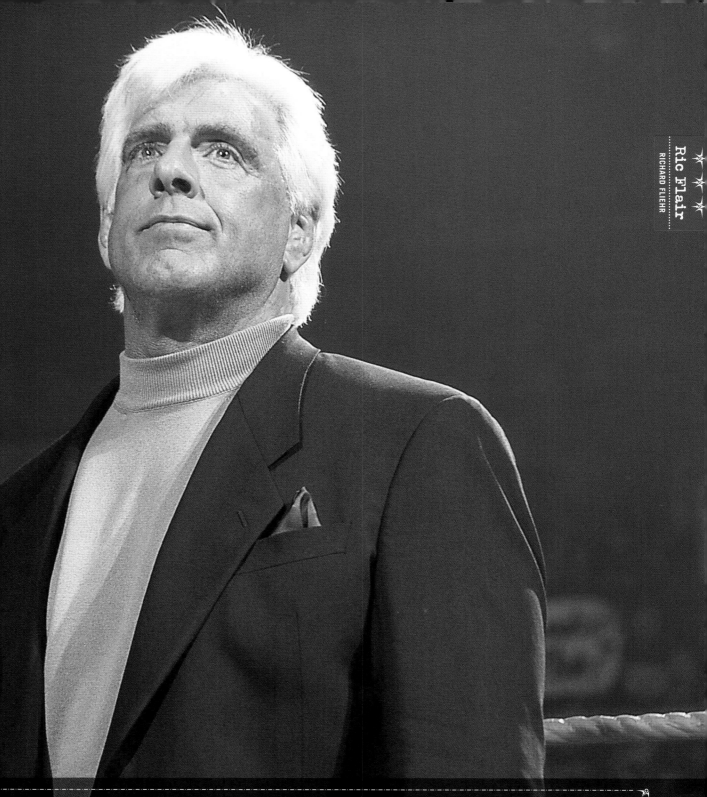

I SEE these biographies on TV about the rock 'n' roll guys, about how hard they live, and it makes me laugh. Those little, skinny, motherfuckers wouldn't have made it through a week with the wrestlers in the '80s. We did the same exact thing they did, except we did it every day of the year and we didn't travel on those lavish, custom buses that they have. We got in a Cadillac or whatever we had, drove 500 miles, got there, wrestled, started drinking, got to bed about 4 o'clock in the morning, got up, worked out, drove about 500 more, talked about everything in the world on the way there, and then did it all over again. Let Mick Jagger and his guys hang around with Roddy Piper. Piper would lay 'em all down to rest. He would kiss 'em all on the forehead as he tucked them in. Let them bring their hardest hitter of all time,

and Roddy would be slapping him upside the face, going, "Wake up! Wake up! Can't go to sleep yet! Can't go to sleep yet! Get up!"

I used to love the car travel, but not anymore. I loved it when I was drinking 20 beers a night, laughing and carrying on, believe it or not, that's when I used to get real creative, thinking up stuff. I don't drink as much anymore; I drink very little. I do enjoy traveling with the guys I know, like Triple H, but now it's more of a job. The guys like to hear me tell the old stories, but I like to tell them now when we're sitting in first class on an airplane instead of driving 300 miles in a car. I told Triple H, he doesn't drink, that if I'd met him 20 years ago, he'd be drinking big-time.

WHEN YOU START OUT, IT'S LIKE, "I WANT TO WORK TO PAY MY BILLS AND THEN I WANT TO HOPEFULLY BUY A HOUSE." AND THEN FOR ME IT WENT TO BUYING MY MOM AND DAD A HOUSE, AND THEN TO BUYING EVERYTHING I WANTED. I REACHED A POINT A COUPLE OF YEARS AGO THAT WHEN I WENT IN THE RING FOR A MATCH OR GOT ON THE MICROPHONE, I WAS ABLE TO SOLELY CONCENTRATE ON JUST BEING AN ARTIST AND NOT WORK FOR THE MONEY. ONCE THAT HAPPENED FOR ME, THINGS JUST REALLY BLEW UP.

I WAS ABLE TO TAKE THINGS TO ANOTHER LEVEL THAT I DIDN'T ANTICIPATE AND I DON'T THINK THE INDUSTRY ANTICIPATED.

THE FANS of our industry are extremely savvy. At the end of the day, they understand the business is a work. It's entertainment, nothing more. If you do things right, you can lose your match and still come out on top. So many times, I've been beaten yet came out the winner. I've passed the torch to Brock Lesnar, Bill Goldberg, Kurt Angle, Chris Jericho — I can't even think of everybody. My mentality is: "I'm gonna get beat tonight, right in the middle of the ring, clean — but I guarantee they'll never forget The Rock after tonight." The people who show up to watch this stuff want to see good versus evil, and they want to let their hair down, and they want to have a good time. Those of us that do this should never forget that, or have illusions that we're anything but what we are, which are entertainers. I could go on forever about this. I love this shit.

I think anybody in the entertainment business that's being honest with you will tell you that they've thought about the people not reacting to them anymore. I've been nervous a few times. After my neck surgery, I was gone for a year. Years before that, I had to take a four-month break when I got dropped on my head and bruised my spinal cord. When you go back in front of that crowd, it's like, "Hey, will I be accepted again? It's gonna be yes or no. Once I got popular, it was all or nothing; you don't ever fight for middle ground if you're trying to draw big money. So, yeah, you get nervous. "Are they still gonna like me? Are they gonna take me back?" A year off in this business can be career suicide. But I've been fortunate enough to build up a fan base that loves me to death. And I love them to death, and I appreciate everything they've done for me. They always take me back, and that goes very much appreciated for me.

"HEY, WILL I BE ACCEPTED AGAIN?" IT'S GONNA BE
YES OR NO.

ONE OF the things I miss about pro wrestling from the days of old is that it wasn't just a business for guys that are all muscled-up. You had Dusty Rhodes, an obviously overweight guy, but a hell of an athlete and a great, charismatic entertainer — one of my all-time favorites. There was Jake "The Snake" Roberts, 6'4", 6'5", but an A-frame, didn't go to the gym, smoked cigarettes and drank a lot. You had Ted DiBiase — he wasn't a muscle guy, either. And "Cowboy" Bob Orton. These were all top guys, they were all distinct personalities. These days, everybody is a bodybuilder. Everybody wants to be jacked-up, and the biggest jacked-up guy is gonna get the biggest push. That's kinda the mentality that's going on right now. I'm not running down the future for a wrestler; I'm just pretty much saying that's the way it is. But I do miss the different shapes and sizes of the days of old. I think that society being what it is, the business being what it is, you're never gonna see another Dusty Rhodes come along and get over and draw big money.

With everybody nowadays coming in looking like a bodybuilder, in some ways that's made it easier for me to identify with people. Here's this beer-swillin', trash-talkin', middle-finger, anti-authority redneck — and he's not a bodybuilder. Everybody could be like me. You see a lot of shaved heads and goatees, and stuff like that. I'm glad that I am just what I am — it turned out to work good for me.

PEOPLE ASK,
"HOW DOES IT FEEL TO BE A WOMAN IN A MAN'S FIELD?"

I DON'T FEEL THAT WAY ANYMORE. I BELIEVE THAT THE WOMEN ADD JUST AS MUCH TO THE SHOWS AS THE MEN DO. BOTH MEN AND WOMEN ENJOY WATCHING US. THE WOMEN LIKE US BECAUSE WE ARE GREAT ROLE MODELS FOR THEM. WE'RE STRONG; WE'RE VERY DEDICATED TO WHAT WE DO; WE BELIEVE IN OURSELVES; WE GO FOR WHAT WE WANT IN LIFE; WE'VE MADE A MARK IN THIS WORLD FOR OURSELVES.

I THINK one of the issues I had in the past was that I looked too far ahead. Now I'm just taking one day at a time and enjoying my life, relishing in the moment. I've been given a second opportunity to be a part of this incredibly wonderful company, and I am just so enjoying it. Years from now, I would still like to be a part of the company, whether it's in marketing or promotions, or as a television personality. I have been given the opportunity to be the first woman in the business to walk down a lot of roads, and hopefully I will be given that opportunity again in the future.

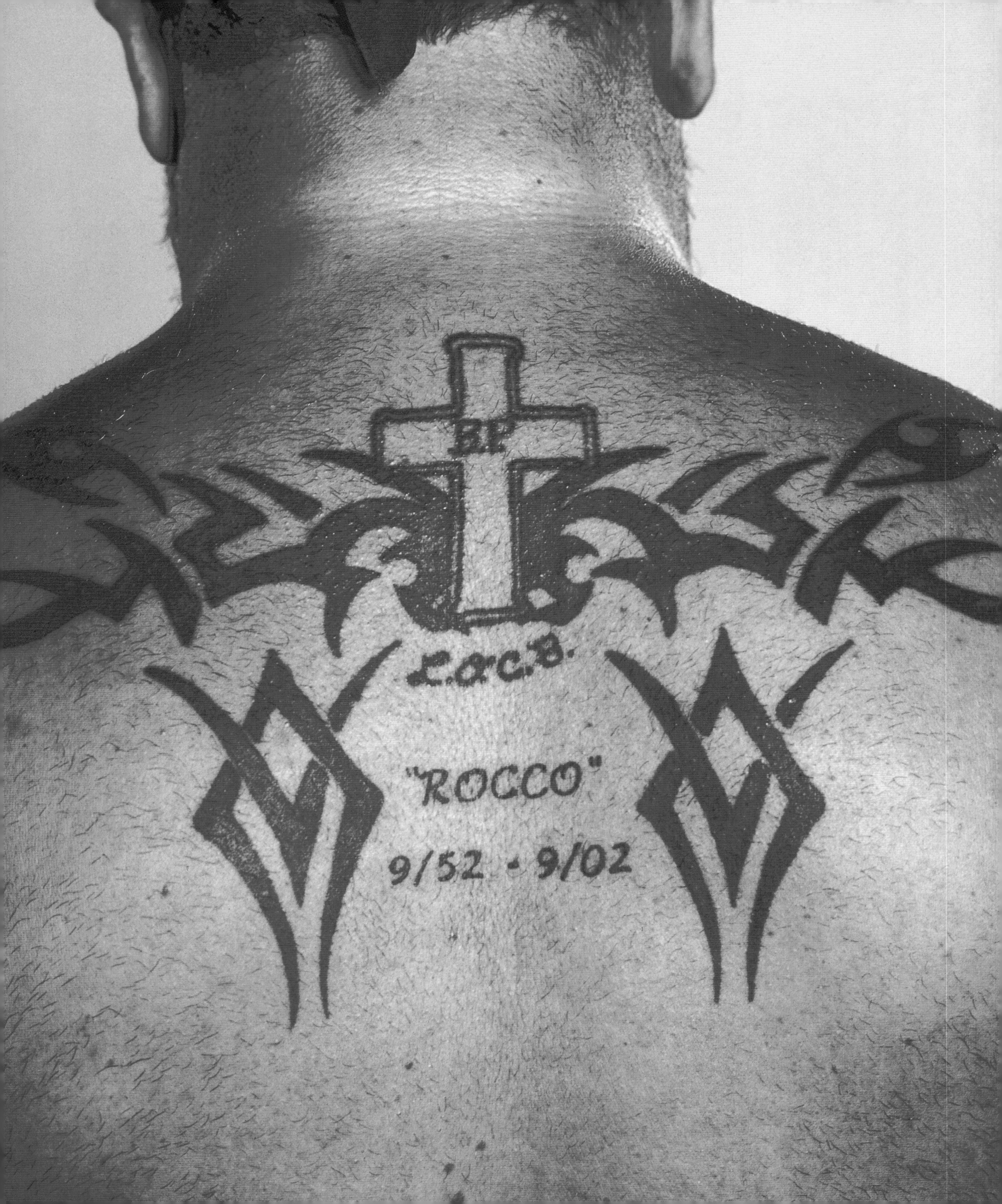

B.P.
L.A.C.B.
"ROCCO"
9/52 - 9/02

SECTION IV

HOME

Shane McMahon

MY WIFE Marissa and I love living in Manhattan. For us, the city has an energy and a vibe unlike anywhere in the world. We take advantage of everything the city has to offer from the theatre to museums and art galleries, to new restaurants and events at Madison Square Garden. We love that you can walk everywhere in New York and there is always something new to discover. The best of everything is in the city, and you don't need a car to get there. On the weekends we wake up and take our dog Medfield to the dog park or sit outside at a café with a cup of coffee and the paper and just let the day take us where it does. Marissa and I are proud to be New Yorkers and to live in, what we believe is the greatest city in the world. We couldn't imagine living anywhere else. Every night when I drive home from work I cross the bridge that leads into Manhattan and my heart begins to race with excitement. I can see the Statue of Liberty in the distance and I say hello. She is a reminder of how much I love New York and how close I am to getting home to see my wife.

I bought a Ram 1500 four-by-four with big tires for myself. Well, my wife took one look at it, and the next thing I knew, her hairbrush was in it, her shoes were in it, and it smelled like Christian Dior perfume. Now, she's got that, and the Escalade, which I don't really fit in, and the Corvette. So I had to go get something for myself for everyday driving. I bought the Ram 2500 with a V-10 — that's one big truck, big enough for even me. Nice wide seats, great head room, great shoulder room. And with that V-10, it really gets up and goes. There's nothing worse than trying to merge into traffic and have somebody just flat outrun you and run you off the road.

THE ABILITY TO STEP ON THE GAS AND GO WHERE YOU WANT TO GO,
that's part of being an American and part of being free.

I'VE DRIVEN so many pieces of crap in my life because I was broke and didn't have any money. I had a 1983 Buick Riviera that the transmission broke down on me at Kmart, and I had to leave the car because I didn't even have enough money to tow it. I drove a beat-up Aspen station wagon that had four bullet holes in it and a bent wheel. So when I got some money, I decided to get some of the cars I always wanted.

My 1971 Cuda convertible has a 440-6 pack and a Pistol Grip four-speed. It's deep-fired blue on the outside, with black interior. There were only 16 of them made. It was restored when I got it. I just love to sit in the garage and look at it; I'd wanted that car since I was 12 years old.

I've got a 1971 Dodge Super Bee that was one of 64 made. It's got a 440-6 pack, slapstick automatic transmission and a 410 Dana positraction rear end. This was a quarter-mile car back in the 1970s. I had the engine rebuilt, and now it's well over 500 horsepower. All the tricks I could put under the hood without making it too gaudy, I did. It's got a top-of-the-line Be Cool radiator, a serpentine belt system, and the heads have been done right. I've got a good stereo system in it, but you know what? I drive it with the radio off, because I just love to hear the engine through the header pipes — it's the best throaty sound. That Super Bee smells old, it feels old, and it reminds me of when I was younger and worked on cars with my dad. Everybody says you have memories according to smell, and those older cars for me have a pleasant smell and remind me of when I was young and with my dad, before he was gone.

I LOVE TO PLAY GOLF.

I LOVE SMASHING THE SHIT OUT OF THAT LITTLE WHITE BALL.

Great therapy. When my back's feeling good and my cleats are dug in, I'm knocking the cover off of it, smacking it straight down the middle, 300 yards easy, no hook, no slice. I can go out there and play, and for four hours the phone doesn't ring, nobody bothers me. I'm out there with three other guys that are friends. It's not beer drinking and crap like that. It's just trying to hit good shots. It only takes one to bring you back again, one true shot in 18 holes. I might shoot 120, but damn it, I birdied that one hole, so I'm coming back.

IF YOU LIVE AND BREATHE THIS BUSINESS 24 HOURS A DAY, SEVEN DAYS A WEEK, IT'LL DRIVE YOU CRAZY. IT'S VERY UNHEALTHY, BECAUSE OUR WORLD IS A PREFABRICATED FANTASY WORLD WHERE WE ALL PLAY CHARACTERS.

IF SOMEBODY STARTS BELIEVING THEIR CHARACTER IS A REAL-LIFE PERSON, THAT'S WHEN PROBLEMS START. WHEN I'M CHRIS JERICHO, IT'S AT THE ARENA, IT'S DURING THE MATCH, THE FOUR DAYS A WEEK I'M ON THE ROAD. WHEN I COME HOME, CHRIS IRVINE COMES OUT. IT'S THE SAME THING WITH MUSIC AND FOZZY. I PLAY MY CHARACTERS WHEN THE TIME IS RIGHT, BUT WHEN I GO HOME AND MY WIFE TELLS ME TO TAKE OUT THE GARBAGE AND I TELL HER, "NO. I'M THE UNDISPUTED WORLD CHAMPION AND A HUGE ROCK STAR." SHE'LL TELL ME TO GO TO HELL AND TAKE THE GARBAGE WITH ME.

WHEN I GO HOME, I'M JUST THE GUY NEXT DOOR, ONLY DIFFERENCE BEING THAT MY JOB IS WRESTLING. IF I HAD TIME TO MOW MY OWN LAWN, I WOULD, BUT I'M NOT HOME ENOUGH TO BE ABLE TO DO EVEN THAT. I WOULD STILL PAY SOMEONE TO CLEAN MY POOL, THOUGH. I USED TO HAVE TO DO THAT WHEN I WAS A KID, AND I HATED IT THEN AND I HATE IT NOW.

I'VE ALWAYS SAID I WANT TO BE ABLE TO ROLL AROUND WITH MY KIDS, THROW THE FOOTBALL AROUND, PLAY SOME HOCKEY WITH THEM. THERE ARE MORNINGS WHEN I'LL WAKE UP, ACHING, AND I'LL GO, "HOW MUCH LONGER DO I GOT?" I DON'T KNOW. YOU THINK OF THE LONG-TERM PHYSICAL IMPLICATIONS — BUT NOT WHEN YOU'RE IN THE RING. WHEN YOU'RE OUT THERE, IT'S JUST LIKE ANY OTHER ATHLETE IN HIS SPORT DOING HIS JOB, REGARDLESS OF THE RISKS.

Edge
ADAM COPELAND

WE FLY INTO A TOWN ON SATURDAY, DO A SHOW, DRIVE SATURDAY NIGHT TO A SUNDAY SHOW, DRIVE SUNDAY NIGHT TO A MONDAY SHOW, DRIVE MONDAY NIGHT, DO *SMACKDOWN!* ON TUESDAY, AND FLY HOME WEDNESDAY. USUALLY IT'S JUST TORRIE AND ME IN THE CAR.

If anybody else needs a ride, we'll take them, but we like to go on our own because we have our routine set. Some people like to get up at six in the morning and train; not us. We sleep in, then train and do whatever else. I like to drive at night, so a lot of times we're not getting to a town until two in the morning. I'm always wide-awake after the show, so it's nice to get the trip out of the way then. After your match, you're so pumped up physically and emotionally, especially if it was a good match. And if it was a bad match, it could be a big downer for you. Either way, you need time to unwind.

Another reason we like to travel alone is because we see these people so much. Everybody usually works out at the same gym. If there's a Cracker Barrel in the area, everyone likes to go there because it's decent food at a good rate. And then you're at the arena all day long with them. To travel with them, too, sometimes gets to be a little much. You see these people more than you see anybody else. Don't get me wrong:

Sometimes five guys traveling in a minivan can be a great time.

BUT SOMETIMES YOU JUST NEED SOME DOWNTIME.

I WAS NOT ALLOWED TO DATE THE WRESTLERS,
OR ANYONE ELSE IN THE COMPANY, ACROSS THE BOARD

— it was completely taboo. With Hunter [Triple H] and I, my dad saw it happening, even when we didn't realize it was happening. He gave us permission to see each other and then he took it away. We only had permission for about a month, and we really started to have strong feelings for each other, and then that was taken away from us and we weren't allowed to see each other. My father just thought it wasn't the right time; he did what he thought was right for business. It was very hard to accept, but I actually thought it was the right thing to do. Hunter said to me at that time, "If it's meant to be, it'll be." And the feelings between us didn't stop, obviously.

WHEN I'M AT HOME, I LIKE TO DO ANYTHING THAT REQUIRES NO ENERGY.
I JUST BUILT MY HOME, AND I REALLY MADE A POINT OF MAKING IT ALL-INCLUSIVE.

I HAVE a gym downstairs; I have a hot tub room; I have a movie room. I have a ton of board games that I can play. I really just take myself away from everything and get away from the whirl-wind situation that my job is. I hardly ever go out; I'm like a hermit — it's almost ridiculous. With food and other things I need around the house, I make one big shopping trip so I don't have to go that much. At home, I'm there to just chill.

After going through what I've gone through, maybe almost dying several times and being on the scrap heap and coming back, I don't really look too forward. I just take everything that comes and enjoy what it is at the time. It's no good wishing your life away on things. Well, I suppose it's OK if you haven't lived your dream; I have. I just get on with what I'm getting on with, and whatever comes up I'll deal with it.

I have a wife and three boys at home. I don't really feel like I miss out too much because I probably spend more time with my children than most people do with theirs. The three days I'm at home, from the time they get home from school starting at 2:30 in the afternoon, I'm here for them. A lot of people that have regular jobs, they come home, they go play golf, they're out and about, they have a lot less time with their children than I do. I think it's the quality of the time you spend with them that's important, more so than just being there every day. And they're always a phone call away if they need anything.

William Regal

DARREN MATTHEWS

HOW LONG WILL I DO THIS?

I think it's more of a question of how long it will let me. If I'm not actually active in the ring, I think I've proven myself as a character that still can be valuable to the company. Just the other day, someone said I should start doing that WWE commissioner-thing again. Basically it was my choice to get out from doing that, the reason being not wanting people to start saying they were sick of seeing it. Everybody liked him; I never had one complaint about it. So this was the time to get away from it, before everybody got a bit fed up with it. If I broke my leg in 20 places, I could go back to doing that tomorrow, whereas a lot of guys would be stuck at home doing nothing. So I can't see why there wouldn't be a role for me in that respect, or just helping out. I've got 20 years of experience doing this.

IT TOOK ME A LONG TIME TO FIGURE OUT HOW TO HAVE A NORMAL LIFE.

The Undertaker

MARK CALLOWAY

MY LIFE for nine years was all wrestling; everything was centered on wrestling. I loved it. I wore all black, even at home. I was always the Undertaker; Mark was never around. Now, I've got the two separated. It took me a long time to figure it out. My wife helped me with that quite a bit. It took meeting her to actually be happy away from this, to find out there was something more to life than wrestling and being on the road. I used to be a wild partyer. I lived the life, I definitely lived the life. I didn't leave too much for the imagination.

It really is hard to have a healthy relationship. You're out there on the road, you're a celebrity, you're exposed to so many different things, people are always telling you how wonderful you are, and you're presented with so many challenges.

If you are a male wrestler, you have your wife — or girlfriend — at home, taking care of the house, sitting there by herself, bringing up kids, wondering what's going on on the road. In that situation, an imagination can run wild, and it usually does. People aren't stupid — they know what's available out there.

There are a lot of guys that do keep monogamous, honest relationships, and that's great. I'm one of those guys now. Back in the day, though, I was the devil. My wife Sara has made an incredible difference in my life and, as a result, in my career. I give her all the credit, not only as a personal motivator, but as somebody that actually makes me happy. Makes me happy without liquor, without any kind of drugs, anything. I didn't ever think that person existed.

I STARTED COLLECTING MICKEY MANTLE MEMORABILIA MANY YEARS AGO.

He was a small-town Oklahoma boy that had some God-given talent and he took advantage of the opportunity and his skills and he made it all the way to New York City. I grew up in a little town called Westville, Oklahoma, and Mickey Mantle grew up in Commerce, Oklahoma. We were both in the northeast corner of the state, probably as the crow flies about an hour away from each other. I was born in 1952, and he was a rookie with the Yankees in 1951, so from the time I was 4 years old, all the Oklahoma news regarding major league baseball was always head-lined by how The Mick did. I don't think New York fans realize how many Yankees fans to this day live in Oklahoma.

EVERY KID ON A LITTLE LEAGUE TEAM WANTED TO BE NUMBER SEVEN, AND IT WAS ALWAYS RESERVED FOR THE BEST PLAYER ON THE TEAM.

I'LL ADMIT: I NEVER WORE NUMBER 7.

I MET MICKEY MANTLE

ON A SOUTHWEST AIRLINES FLIGHT ONE TIME FROM DALLAS TO TULSA.

HE WAS ON HIS WAY THERE TO DO A BASEBALL CARD SIGNING, AND I WAS
ON MY WAY THERE TO REFEREE A HIGH SCHOOL FOOTBALL GAME.
WE SAT BESIDE EACH OTHER, AND WE HAD A REAL COOL CONVERSATION.
I REMEMBER HE STILL LOOKED FIT, BUT HIS FACE LOOKED OLD. HE HAD THOSE
GREAT SHOULDERS AND UPPER ARMS, AND HIS FOREARMS WERE LIKE POPEYE'S.
IT WAS A 45-MINUTE FLIGHT, AND HE HAD THREE SCREWDRIVERS. THE FLIGHT
ATTENDANTS AT THE TIME WERE WEARING KHAKI SHORTS,
AND I REMEMBER THE MICK TOOK A PARTICULAR LIKING TO ONE OF THEM.

I OWN A 1951 MICKEY MANTLE BOWMAN ROOKIE CARD,

PROBABLY 10 AUTOGRAPHED BASEBALLS, BATS, GLOVES, CAPS, AND JERSEYS OF
HIS, AND EVERY SPORTS ILLUSTRATED COVER HE WAS EVER ON, AUTOGRAPHED.
BUT I WAS SO AWESTRUCK SITTING NEXT TO HIM ON THAT AIRPLANE THAT I DIDN'T
HAVE THE COURAGE TO ASK HIM FOR AN AUTOGRAPH. I'VE ALWAYS THOUGHT THAT
EVEN THOUGH I DIDN'T GET AN AUTOGRAPH THAT DAY — I'VE GOT PLENTY OF
MICKEY MANTLE AUTOGRAPHS IN MY COLLECTION THAT I BOUGHT AND PAID
FOR — WHAT I DO HAVE IS A 45-MINUTE PLANE RIDE THAT GAVE ME

MEMORIES THAT ARE GONNA LAST A LIFETIME.

I'VE BEEN DEER HUNTING PROBABLY SINCE I WAS ABOUT 13. My dad is a lifelong deer hunter, and he got me and my brothers all hunting. Two years ago, I didn't hunt except maybe one day; the new WWE schedule was so demanding, I just didn't have time to hunt. This past year, with everything that happened, I had a lot of time to hunt, so I went a lot, and I actually killed two very nice white-tail deer, one of the most elusive, smartest animals that you can hunt in North America, probably the number one big trophy animal. I also do a lot of dove hunting and a little bit of turkey hunting. Don't really do any quail hunting —

I don't have a dog. How much relaxation I get all depends on how long the trip is. It'll take me at least a day and a half to realize that I don't have to go back to work for a couple days, and then I can kind of deprogram and actually be relaxed. I won't hunt with just anybody because I'm always safety-minded. I'll usually only hunt with my friends. We're real safe about what we do. Don't get me wrong: We have a blast around the campfire at night, cookin' and drinkin' beer, but we're responsible, too. **HUNTING IS ONE OF THE MOST RELAXING THINGS THAT I CAN DO, SOMETHING THAT I'LL DO FOR THE REST OF MY LIFE.**

IT'S VERY difficult in our business to keep a relationship going. Females are difficult to deal with, as it is. Most of them don't understand what we go through on the road, as far as being in the ring; dealing with the fans, living out of a suitcase, always having to catch a plane, looking for a decent place to eat late at night, waiting around for 8 hours to do a 15-minute shoot, and the stress that's involved all day. Most women think, "You're on the road; you're being glamorized; there's a lot of women around," and that causes problems. Yeah, there's a lot of stuff available to you on the road — if that's what you're going for. If you don't have a stable life, a stable household, chances are you're gonna be screwed up. I've seen a lot of guys' lives get screwed up in this business, and a lot of them are six feet under right now, God rest their souls.

I'm in a really good relationship now with Sharmell. I think part of the reason for it is because she's been in the business and she knows what we go through. Sharmell knows what I'm doing out there, and I feel like she understands why I'm driving myself the way I am. I do it now, so we can have all our time together later.

I WON'T RAISE A KID WHEN I'M ON THE ROAD EVER AGAIN.

You can do it, but it's not going to be done right; there's gonna be a lot of aftereffects.

I'm going through that right now with my son. I was 17 when he was born, and I got custody of him when he was 6 years old. I just wanted to raise him and do the right thing, just try to be a good father. But we're not together right now because of a lot of baggage. Because I've been on the road for 13 years, I missed out on a lot of things. I tried to be there for as much as I could, but when you're a kid, you don't understand that.

YOU JUST KNOW,

"DAD IS NOT HERE AGAIN TONIGHT. WHY DOES DAD HAVE TO BE ON THE ROAD SO MUCH? WHY DOES EVERYBODY HAVE TO COME UP TO MY DAD AND WANT AUTOGRAPHS? WHY CAN'T MY DAD COME TO THE GAMES AND SIT DOWN AND WATCH ME PLAY BALL?"

I WANT TO BE WITH MY SON, BUT HE'S GOT A LOT OF ANGER TOWARDS ME RIGHT NOW.

WRESTLING WAS JUST SOMETHING THAT FELL INTO MY HANDS, I HAD NO IDEA WHAT I WAS REALLY GETTING MYSELF INTO.

I FELT LIKE IT WAS A HOBBY. I DIDN'T LOOK AT IT AS A CAREER, I REALLY DIDN'T THINK YOU COULD MAKE A LOT OF MONEY DOING IT. IT WASN'T SOMETHING I EVER THOUGHT ABOUT DOING THAT WOULD GET ME TO WHERE I AM TODAY.

It was something I had watched on television as a kid, but it wasn't something I had dreamed about or thought about doing ever in a million years. My brother had always wanted to be a professional wrestler, and he had been talking for a long time to this guy, Ivan Putsky, who kept saying he was going to open a wrestling school. When he finally did, my brother came to me and said, "Hey, man, do you want to try this out with me?" I was 25 years old, just struggling along, working in the warehouse at American Mini Storage, just trying to survive, just me and my son coming up in life, just trying to keep a roof over our heads, no plans or ambitions as far as what I wanted to be in life. So if it could benefit me, I thought, "Hey, I'll try it out." But it was $3,000 to go, and I didn't have it. So my boss at that time, he sponsored me to go to wrestling school.

FIVE YEARS ago, I stopped wrestling because I needed back surgery. So the traveling and being out every night on the road, being out on the town, stopped. But I was still not in a good place in my life. Then I met Rebecca, who was sent to me by God, and a year after we were married, our son was born. But I still wrestled a few demons that kept me from being all that I could be as a husband and a father. I was trying and trying, but I couldn't do it by myself. Then one Christmas, my wife left a study Bible and a book called "Straight Talk" to men under the tree for me. The book was by Dr. James Dobson, who is a Christian psychologist. I read it and I found just how desperately short I was falling. I think I was probably better than 70, 80 percent of the husbands and fathers. By the world's standards, I was doing OK, but by God's standards, I was far, far short of what he expected from my life. I read a couple more books on that, and I started to read that Bible. I was raised Catholic, but I didn't know about salvation, about being born again, and my wife — she's a Biblical woman — just sort of let me find out on my own. One day, I walked into Cornerstone Church and asked them if they could set me up with Bible study. This guy peeked his head outside of his door and said, "You can come to mine." So that Wednesday I went to his house for Bible study and he said, "Have you said the Sinner's Prayer?" And I said, "No. I've said a lot of prayers, but I don't remember the name of that one." And he said, "Well, have you been born again?" And I said, "No. I've heard that term, but I've been born just the once." He said, "Well, say this with me." And I said the Sinner's Prayer with him, and I wept like a baby, and from that day on I have lived by the guidelines that God puts forward to me as a man in the Bible. My outlook physically and spiritually from that day has changed and has done nothing but get better ever since. Everything that was once there in my life is gone, and it wasn't even a struggle. I was never really a drinker, but I've never touched a drink since. I found out last week that some of the supplements I was taking had ephedra in them — it was in the news that that stuff was linked to a baseball player's death — and I threw them all out.

ONCE I REALIZED THAT THE HOLY SPIRIT AND GOD'S SON ARE
LIVING IN MY BODY AND THAT MY BODY IS A TEMPLE,

I WON'T DO ANYTHING TO COMPROMISE MY HEALTH.

Shawn Michaels
MICHAEL HIGGENBOTTOM

I AM MARRIED - VERY HAPPILY MARRIED. It IS DIFFICULT to HAVE A RELATIONSHIP IN THIS BUSINESS, BUT At the SAME TIME, At LEAST FOR ME, it'S DIFFICULT to NOT HAVE A RELATIONSHIP AND BE IN THIS BUSINESS. I'VE BEEN DOING THIS PROFESSIONALLY SINCE 1990, AND I HAD MY TIMES BEING SINGLE AND HAVING FUN ON THE ROAD. NOW, I NEED SOMEBODY to GO HOME to, AND I HAVE ONE OF THOSE RELATIONSHIPS THAT ALL THE OTHER COUPLES ENVY. MY WIFE AND I GET ALONG GREAT; WE'RE BEST FRIENDS. I USED to FEEL LIKE ALL THE OTHER WRESTLERS WANTED to BE ME, AND THEN I FOUND A WIFE THAT IS A GREAT MATCH, AND NOW I THINK ALL THE OTHER COUPLES WANT to BE US. SHE KNEW NOTHING ABOUT WRESTLING WHEN I MET HER, AND I TOOK HER RIGHT INTO MY WORLD. I HAD HER COME to THE SHOWS; I HAD HER SEE WHAT I DO IN THE RING, WHICH COMPLETELY SHOCKED HER, ESPECIALLY BACK THEN At ECW. I TOOK HER ON THE ROAD BECAUSE I WANTED HER to SEE ALL THE CRAZY STUFF THAT GOES ON, ALL THE STUFF THAT'S OUT THERE THAT WOULD CONCERN A WIFE.

SHE WAS STILL AROUND AFTER ALL THAT, SO I KNEW WE HAD A GOOD CHANCE TO MAKE IT TOGETHER.

With Matt, I love the traveling. I don't like it by myself, because it's very lonely and very aggravating. The smallest little thing, like trying to find something to eat when you land in a town and it's late, can be really annoying. Or trying to find a gym when you have an hour and a half to work out, which should be plenty of time, but it takes you 55 minutes to find the gym because you got wrong directions. But if you're traveling with friends and family that you love, which is what I consider Matt and Jeff, then you can laugh at it or find something positive about it.

I THINK Matt and I will stay together, but we're not in any hurry to get married. Whenever the time is right — I'm not worrying about it. I guess in a romantic way, I'd like to have an actual wedding — not have to have my black gear bag in the trunk, get married, and hop in the car and go to the airport for the next show.

Right now, I'm in the best relationship I've ever been in. I think the majority of that is the person I'm with; the other part of it is having so much in common.

Matt and I were able to be on the road together for a while, and that's such a bonding experience. But after I got hurt, I went from traveling with Matt and being at home together with him to where I felt like I rarely saw him. Getting seriously injured and being at home by myself, I felt so incredibly alone. I was completely by myself for a good while, and I couldn't drive, couldn't do a lot of simple stuff on my own. No personal feelings against Matt, but I felt very, very alienated. It was the toughest time emotionally I've ever had to deal with.

I wouldn't say I'm an animal rights activist; I'm more of an activist of educating people on the serious pet overpopulation problem in the United States. Granted, there are a million other issues that are important, such as terminally ill children or disease. I feel as if most of America lives with an "out of sight, out of mind" mentality. To change anything, somebody needs to make people aware of the problems that exist. Currently, every person in America would have to own 14 animals to fix the overpopulation problem, and for the next generation to have to own 7 would mean neutering all the animals. I started volunteering at the shelter to give some relief to the people that are so dedicated to doing this emotionally taxing job. Nobody gets into the animal shelter business for money. I want to do what I can to help raise awareness. Growing up, I worked at kennels, animal hospitals, and grooming shops. I pretty much worked at those places, until minimum wage didn't pay my bills anymore. I love animals, but never was allowed to have them growing up. Well, never allowed to have the one pet I wanted, a dog.

I'M AN ANIMAL PERSON,

BUT ULTIMATELY I'M A DOG PERSON.

Lita
AMY DUMAS

I'm very proud that Shane and Steph wanted to be in the business that we're in, as opposed to me saying, "You're in the business."

SHANE ALWAYS wanted to be in the business, and I didn't know that Steph did, too, but she always did. I told Shane that I wouldn't let him in the business until he graduated from college. He didn't even bother going to his graduation ceremony. He had his car all packed up, finished his last exam, drove down that same day, and the next day went to work. I said, "Don't you want to go to the ceremony?" He said, "Nope, I want to start to work. You said as soon as I graduated college, I could go to work." With Steph, I had a meeting the summer after her junior year of college and said, "OK, you have to really get serious. What do you want to be? What do you want to do with your life?" And she

You're lucky to have the job. If you can find another job somewhere that's gonna give you more money, fine, Shane. But meanwhile, don't bother me." So the little bastard went out and found a job paying him twice as much as I was paying him — it broke my heart. He got a job as a brickmason's laborer; he actually helped build our house. I outsmarted myself on that one. On the one hand, I was so proud of him because he went out and found a job on his own that paid him more money. On the other hand, I thought, "Damn, you idiot, Vince; you're driving him away."

To see them enjoy this business as much as they do gives me a sense of

looked at me like I'm such a dummy, and she said, "I just want to work in the business with you guys. That's all I've ever wanted to do."

During the summers and every holiday, they always worked — I felt they should earn their spending money and know what that's like. They didn't have to work in the company, but they always did. They didn't get any special treatment. Whatever minimum wage was, that's what they got paid. Shane had been working in the warehouse in the summertime, and he came to me one year — he was 16 or 17 — and said, "Dad, I'm been doing this for three years now, and I really think I'm due a raise." I said, "A raise, my ass. You don't get a raise.

gratification that I don't think I could get if they were working for someone else. My grandfather was in the business, my dad was in the business, I'm in the business, and now Shane and Steph are in the business, and chances are that some of their children are gonna want to be in this business. There's a sense of gratification in that — it's not an immortality thing, but it gives you reason, it gives you purpose for each succeeding generation. Some of their kids could be like the Firestone family and just live off of their pension and not want it. And others will be like, "We gotta have it!" Maybe all of them will be that way, and they'll be fighting amongst each other.

I'll be looking up - not looking down and smiling and enjoying the fracas, I'm sure.

When I left Japan, I stayed in Puerto Rico for 6 months. I was thinking about moving to Boston, but it's very expensive to live there, and it's cold and snows a lot. I was thinking also about Florida, but there's too much humidity, same as Puerto Rico. Stone Cold Steve Austin told me that Texas was the best, and he said I should look at San Antonio. I listen to Stone Cold. He's my favorite. My children are learning the American ways, and they like the television programs here. My wife misses Japan, but we have a telephone and she can call. I like the United States—maybe I'll live here forever. We still like Japanese food the best, but we are finding the barbecue chicken and beef to be very delicious.

In a normal week, I get home on Wednesday afternoon. By the time I get home, I'm usually pretty tired. I'll go through my mail, write out bills, stuff like that, but mostly I just kind of curl up in the house. Thursday, I try to get all my maintenance done: nails, hair, a facial, all that. That usually takes me half a day, at least. Then it's shopping. If I have a Bra and Panties match coming up, I have to go get a new bra and panties, or whatever it is. And I like to have a different outfit every week for the shows. We're responsible for our own costumes, which I like, because I love fashion and being creative, picking my own costumes and embellishing them. I love doing anything where I can be creative. I like to sew, and shopping is a huge passion for me, which is kind of bad. Friday is our day for just kicking back, going someplace, doing something fun. It's probably our only day of the week that would be considered normal by most people's standards. But we have to leave the next day, so we're starting to pack again.

WHEN I FIRST STARTED, I HAD NO IDEA THAT I COULD EVER BE WHERE I AM TODAY. NOBODY COULD DREAM THAT, BECAUSE THE BUSINESS AT THAT TIME DIDN'T HAVE THE MONEY IN IT THAT IT HAS NOW.

I just knew that I liked it a lot, and I knew that I got along with the guys, and I knew that I had found a niche in life. I've got a tremendous gift that someone's given me. I have been very, very lucky. I've gotten a lot more than I could have asked for. There's nothing left for me to do; I have done it all. It's not like my wife and I are gonna retire and travel around the world, we've done that. There's nothing left for us to do, except be comfortable. We've been to every country 10 times, from Japan to Singapore from Europe to Honolulu. And we did it when we were healthy and could have a good time, and they're great memories. My mom and dad saved a lot of money, and now they've lost a lot of it because of the stock market. I just wished they had lived it. My mom is sick now, and my dad has passed away. They were so worried about having money at the end. I'd rather say I did it all, and downsize at the end.

THE SECOND that people found out I was in a legitimate relationship with Stephanie McMahon, I think everybody forgot about anything I had ever accomplished in the business. You would think I had never been a star before I met her. I went from the guy that busted his ass for all those years to get where I wanted to be to the guy that screwed the boss's daughter to get himself in a main-event spot. I was in the main events long before that. At first, it was difficult. We went through a period of time where, while we were not trying to hide it, we tried to tone down the relationship when we were around people in the business. But it didn't take long before I realized, "Hey, fuck that. It's my life. If anybody thinks I'm with her just to get ahead in the business, that's their problem." We talked to Vince about us, and first he said OK, then he changed his mind and said, "I don't think it's good for business; I don't think it's good for you." We said, "Well, let's try to go our separate ways" — but it was just there between us. We couldn't avoid it and couldn't deny it; you can't help who you fall in love with. Vince saw that and said, "I was wrong." So then we started having the relationship again, and it just took off, especially once we stopped trying to make like we weren't together and just lived our lives.